MW00903470

The Legacy: Looking Back While Moving Forward
Second Edition published 2011 by Augusta Books
6 Freda Road
Christchurch, Dorset, BH23 1LY
United Kingdom
www.augustabooks.co.uk
Copyright © 2011 Dr Fredi Jackson
ISBN 1456440861
EAN-13 9781456440862

All rights reserved. No part of this publication may be reproduced in any form or by any means, graphic, electronic or mechanical, including photocopying, recording, taping or information storage and retrieval systems, without the prior permission in writing of the publishers.

The Legacy

Looking Back While Moving Forward

by Dr Fredi Jackson

AVGVSTA)

All thanks and praises to Jesus Christ—my life!

Table of Contents

Forward: The Legacy   ix

Chapter I: Looking Back: The Origin of Humankind   1

Chapter II: The Birth and Genealogy of Jesus Christ   5

Chapter III: Civilization in Africa   19

Chapter IV: The Social Significance of Race and Ethnicity   39

Chapter V: The Re-introduction of Blacks to the Americas (1400-1865)   45

Chapter VI: While Moving Forward: The Black Family After Slavery (1865-Present)   63

Chapter VII: The Black Church—The Black Religion   87

The Conclusion   115

Acknowledgments   135

References   137

Bibliography   145

About the Author   153

Forward: The Legacy

My brother, Robert (Bob) Jackson, once talked about how black ice on the roads is very similar to racism. We know it is out there, but it is not always apparent or visible...

"You know, when black ice is on the roadway, it is very difficult to see regardless of the amount of daylight. For instance on Sunday, in every state in America, there will be White churches having their services and Black churches having theirs—both serving the same God. Sunday morning at 11am is a very 'racist' time in America!"

This was back in 1992, when my brother was Pastor of Acts Full Gospel Church in Oakland, CA. Since then my brother has become Bishop Bob Jackson at the same church.

When I first had the idea for this book, I wanted to tackle the 'black ice' scenario head-on and write about the hidden nature of racism in the United States of America. But as I began researching the history of African Americans the more I needed to discover *why* things are the way they are today. You could say I have been on a journey of discovery. Now, I have drawn on all my experience as a teacher, a mother and a grandmother to bring you my discoveries, along with some 'nuggets of wisdom' that I have picked up along the way. It is my hope that this book will highlight some of the less well known parts of our history, and thereby inspire people of all ethnicities and ages to think again about where they come from and how with God's love we can reconcile the past with the present. This book is *my legacy* to my dear family and friends.

Throughout, I have taken an Afro-centric view on the origins of man—that is to say—the first people in existence were Black African men and women. The current Ethiopian flag is pictured on the front cover as a nod to these beginnings. As the book progresses the story unfolds from this region of Africa. In addition to looking at the Biblical history of the Black people, I will be confronting and grappling with the legacy of racism in the United States of America. We must try and answer challenging questions about the past if we are truly to become "change agents" for the future. Has history been written by 'the victors'? Has politics, driven by racial prejudice, distorted genuine scholarship? The person doing the writing usually writes from his or her own perspective, and seeing as most history has been written by Europeans, do standard textbooks really strive to present an accurate picture of history?

The material used in this book comes from authoritative sources, with excerpts from well-known authors, historians and researchers. Starting at Creation, we will follow African people from Biblical days right up to the 21st Century, looking at many of the struggles African Americans have been through in past and present years. We will consider it a miracle that Black people have survived at all through the most horrendous slavery ever witnessed by humankind. Later on, we will look at some of the inspiring contributions made to the world and to America by Blacks or African Americans, but first and foremost I want to provide a Biblical framework for the beginnings of our race.

In Biblical times and throughout history, various groups have come to dislike each other. The earliest Biblical example can be seen in the original family when Cain, in a fit of jealousy, murdered his brother Abel. Clearly, this hatred had nothing to do with race or skin color. Similarly, as we look back at the epic rivalries and wars between the ancient nations, it is hard to imagine that any of those conflicts had to do with skin color either. Most people in Biblical times lived in the desert and other arid areas. People looked very similar in appearance and complexion, and since mankind came from one source it never would have made sense to discriminate or treat groups differently based on skin tone. Such bigotry was virtually unheard of (as far as we have been able to research) in antiquity. The world began with one man and one woman; all humans can be traced back to Adam and Eve in the Holy Bible. This comes from the first book of Genesis. Whether people choose to believe it or not, all humans are related. Scientific findings have also concluded that humans are related despite their ethnic origin. Humans share the same biological components that distinguish Homo sapiens from other species of animals: all humans are 98% the same.

Why then, some may ask, do we have so much conflict and strife? There has always been war because there has always been sin—but none of these wars were over the color of skin. Tribal wars erupted based on disputes over territory and resources. The victor would take over the defeated tribe and their possessions. This led to forms of slavery, which were practiced by most Biblical societies. But the slavery of ancient times was very different from the kind practiced in America. In ancient times race was not the primary factor of slavery—which is the exact opposite of American history, where race (or color) laid the foundations for the institution of slavery.

One of the vestiges of slavery, historically, has been the manner in which Black people have had to interact with White people. In the not so distant past, Blacks were taught to be careful of their demeanor in the presence of Whites. Like road signs that cautioned of unsuspected dangers (the 'black ice' scenario), experience taught most southern Blacks to be wary when dealing with Caucasians. Hence came the shuffling of feet, looking down and never looking directly into a White person's face—if one did it could have been taken as a sign of aggression or hostility leading to retribution. For Blacks this form of docility was used in order to protect one's life, because if the White man was angry it was lawful for him to treat Blacks with mild to extreme brutality,even death. Though Blacks were technically free after the Civil War, they were still not treated as equal citizens (not even close) in their own country. This has led to a psychological issue for most Blacks even to the present. A double standard of behavior and treatment was firmly in place; often codified by law, and at the very least segregation was present in the mind-set of some Caucasian people.

By educating themselves in the ways of White people, Blacks managed to avoid many pitfalls; it was a type of survival course young Black men had to go through if they wanted to live. They were indoctrinated into the ways and methods of the White group. This knowledge was passed down from family to family, from generation to generation; ensuring that the ingrained prejudice of Whites would continue unabated. And how could it not? No one was ever taught differently, which is precisely the problem with prejudice. It operates out of sheer ignorance. People fear what is not like them. More broadly, prejudice is a learned behavior for all ethnicities, not just Blacks and Whites. Racism is hard to recognize in America because it comes with many masks. Racism is often excused as being tradition or "the American way" because it is a 'sensitive issue' that most people would prefer to just go away. Of course, this is no solution at all! Discrimination and ignorance are at the heart of prejudice and racism. We have passed legislation to promote equality in American culture; and many people believe that with these new laws in place there are no racial issues left. However, the problem remains.

The truth is, in America, all the legislation in the world cannot begin to change what is in people's hearts. People will not change their entrenched views until they learn and are convinced that what they are doing is wrong. Change in people's heart is the only answer. But hardened hearts, by their very nature, resist change. Therefore, racism has become covert. It is difficult to discern, very much like 'black ice' on the roadways in winter. In America, racism is a problem for most minority groups, and lower economic classes. As long as Americans continue to teach their children prejudice against those who are different from their own group, racism will continue to grow and plague America's citizens. It infects everything it touches. Whether it be individuals, family members, the business world, arts, politics or religion, its ugly tentacles have a sickeningly long reach. Children learn what is said concerning other groups, which they learn first from their parents. The question is, does this kind of racism have to continue into perpetuity? Or is there a way for us to break the chain of ignorance that forges new links with every coming generation? There is hope but it will take a different kind of law and a change of mankind's heart to eradicate this problem. Nothing outside of ourselves can effect such change; it has to come from within. With God's help this change will come about. Americans truly united can make all the difference this country needs. With this challenge comes tremendous opportunity. America may yet live up to her stated ideals of freedom, equality and justice for all!

God awaits America's commitment to alleviate racial problems through faithful adherence to His just laws. As Christians, we can do it! As Americans we must do it! America needs to set an example for the rest of the world. And there is no better place to start than by confronting the realities of history in this great nation by researching and finding the true history as it relates to Africans in a fair, logical and unbiased manner.

Some of the works referenced within the pages of this book will, undoubtedly, be criticized as highly controversial. Yet, controversial does not mean unfounded, and, as often happens, some works on the cutting edge of scholarship are initially rejected only to be later proven correct. Most importantly, it is my hope that readers will obtain knowledge of God's wisdom, which is depicted throughout the Holy Bible—God loves all His children whether they are white, yellow, red, brown, or black. We must be willing to listen to different perspectives if we want to be truly informed. Familiarize ourselves with beliefs that challenge 'Western' tradition so that we can form a balanced picture of how and why we have arrived at this point today. In short, African Americans must find the truth for themselves.

Remembering my brother Robert's words about Sunday being the most segregated day in America (this was in a sermon in 1992, which inspired my planning for *The Legacy*), it is true that Black Christians visiting Caucasian churches have sometimes felt left out of worship services, and vice versa. Most Blacks prefer the energy of Black services, and only small numbers have joined White churches in recent years. I personally feel that the church people attend should be a matter of preference and not based on 'race'. People should go where ever they feel comfortable. Neither the name of the church nor the names of its members are as important as the Word of God and the saving of souls for the Lord.

According to the Bible, God created man in His own image and likeness. Where mankind has failed is by attempting to make God in his image. Mankind has tended to describe God in his likeness; and for centuries that has meant Caucasian. For all these years the portrait of Jesus as a Caucasian has been accepted as 'truth' because it was the only picture of Jesus that had been made. It was an egocentric quest. Happily, in recent years, Afro-centric images have begun to appear more widely in churches. As long as we continue to reach out to one another, across barriers, and respect each other's perspectives there is hope!

A note about racial nomenclature: Throughout this book I have used words interchangeably: Caucasian (White); Black (African American). The word "Negro" will not be used unless it is part of a quote. "Negro" is the Spanish/Portuguese word for "black" derived from Latin. The other N— word will not be used as it too is very debasing, and dangerous. These words have been used when a Black person was being lynched! This word 'negro' came into vogue during the slave trade in an attempt to distinguish the African slaves from Ethiopians or Egyptians which is what their true names were. However, both words 'negro' and 'n—' hold many negative connotations for Blacks throughout American history. Richard B. Moore, in his book *The Name Negro and Its Evil Use,* focused upon the concept of color and race as false divisions of the human race that are used to perpetuate power. Early in life he (Moore) had realized that race had been tied to class by "instituting a segregated society."

Indeed, the segregated society has existed prior to 1896, before it was made law (or de jure). This was the separate but equal doctrine. This segregation lasted until the 1960's when the civil rights laws supposedly dismantled it. There is still (defacto) segregation. Racism still remains a major problem in America!

Let us make man in our own image, according to our likeness
(Genesis 1:26)

Chapter I.

Looking Back:
The Origin of Humankind

The ultraviolet rays from the sun activate melanin, which is a chemical found in human skin. Where you live geographically and how much sun you are exposed to determines your skin color. The more intense the ultraviolet radiation, the darker the skin pigmentation will become. Jesus was probably olive skinned because of where he lived. One could say that, really, there are no 'white' people, there are just very light brown ones (and some of them try their best to get a tan, to look better. What is that all about?) Humankind is made in God's own image. According to Genesis:

> Then God said, "Let us make humankind: in our image, according to our likeness; and let them have dominion over the fish of the sea, and over the birds of the air, and over the cattle, and over the wild animals of the earth." [1]

God was talking to Jesus and the Holy Spirit when He said 'let us make humankind in our image…' Some people may not be aware that the "Three" are One.

> And the Lord God formed man of the dust of the ground, and breathed into his nostrils the breath of life; and man became a living soul. [2]

God, Jesus and the Holy Spirit used the dust of the earth to form man, and God, with the other Master Planners, formed man in Their own image. To go a bit further with this idea, it was probably not 'white dust.' When God, Jesus and the Holy Spirit created man in Their image, man was given dominion over the earth and all its creatures. God blessed man and He made woman from man's rib. God decreed that they should be fruitful. Not long after this came history's first "baby boom."

Genesis identifies four key rivers where the burgeoning human population thrived. They are the Pishon and Gihon rivers, associated with the ancient Hebrew land, Cush (present day Ethiopia); and the Hiddekel (Tigris) and the Euphrates located in southeastern Turkey, which flow into present day Syria and Iraq. [3]

These rivers were the birthplace of humankind. So it is easy to assume, given the arid climate of the region, that the first humans were probably brown skinned. It is important to establish that there was, and is, but one race of people. We all share the same beginnings and evidence points toward humankind evolving from a single family. God created the first man with His own hands and we have all developed according to God's plan. If God had wanted people to look alike, He could have very well performed this task. Without a doubt, diversity has been a key element of the divine plan from the very beginning.

A person's individual prejudices are often rooted in the idea that one race is superior to another, and some use Biblical history to attempt to justify their biases. It seems clear, however, that such people have twisted scriptural facts in an attempt to prop up their own faulty thinking, *'And the whole earth was of one language, and of one speech'* (note: Genesis clearly states that God never created any one group to be superior over any other.

Later, when Moses describes the Table of Nations in Genesis, which lists the lineage of Noah's family, He takes the time to write about a descendant of Cush named Nimrod. He was the first king and the very beginning of the monarchy system. Nimrod was a mighty hunter "blessed by God." He reigned over large areas of land, which included Babel, Erech, Accad, and Calneh in the land of Sinar. Through military campaigns he extended his empire to Assyria. He built Rehoboth-Ir, Calah, and Resen, with the main city of Nineveh as the capital of his empire. The population grew and spread eastward. Fertile land was discovered in the plains of Babylon and it became heavily populated. The people along with their leader Nimrod who lived there began to talk about building a great city with a temple tower that would reach into the heavens. This was to be a proud, eternal monument to themselves and their own ingenuity, independent of God. The people reasoned that this tower would stand so tall they would literally walk into God's Holy Heaven.

> And the Lord said, Behold, the people are one, and they have all one language; and this they begin to do: and now nothing will be restrained from them, which they have imagined to do. And God said, let us go down, and there confound their language, that they may not understand one another's speech. So the Lord scattered them abroad from hence upon the face of all the earth; and they left off to build the city. Therefore is the name of it called Babel; because the Lord did there confound the language of all the earth; and from thence did the Lord scatter them abroad upon the face of all the earth. [4]

This scattering explains why today, we have a variety of cultures, languages, and people of different skin tones all over the world. The original unity no longer existed, because God could not trust mankind to be obedient to Him. Human beings were now widely dispersed throughout the earth. Yet this story from the Bible tells us why this happened—and it has nothing to do with superiority. It was, instead, God's way of teaching an important lesson to mankind: that all of us must rely on God's grace and wisdom for our very lives and what we own. Being disobedient separates people from God; people will then separate themselves from each other as well, leading to ignorance, violence and hatred of those different from themselves.

A scientist studied the possibility of the earth having been one solid land mass. His name was Alfred Wegner and he developed the

'Pangia Theory'. If only he had read The Bible he would have known that the earth started as one landmass, with all the people living to-gether in one place, with the same language—without the need for any scientific investigation!

Behold, a virgin shall be with child, and shall bring forth a son, and they shall call his name Emmanuel, which being interpreted is, God with us
(Matthew 1:23)

Chapter II.

The Birth and Genealogy of Jesus Christ

It is hopefully understood that Jesus and the Holy Spirit were with God the father from the beginning. God, Jesus and The Holy Spirit are the Alpha and the Omega, the beginning and the end! Jesus was in the Garden of Eden with His father when God said, "Let us make man in our image, after our likeness..." God was speaking to the Lord Jesus Christ and the Holy Spirit. Jesus decided to leave heaven to come to Earth as a God/man, to die for the sins of the world. It was the only way that mankind could be redeemed from sin. We are going to look back at Jesus' birth; His Immaculate Conception and His genealogy. Matthew 1-16 describes the lineage of Jesus Christ, the Savior to all, irrespective of ethnicity:

> *The book of generation of Jesus Christ, the son of David, the son of Abraham; Abraham begat Isaac; and Isaac begat Jacob; and Jacob begat Judas and his brethren; and Judas begat Phares and Zara of Thamar; and Phares begat Esrom; and Esrom begat Aram; and Aram Begat Aminadab; and Aminadab begat Naasson; and Naasson begat Salmon; and Salmon begat Booz of Rachab; and Boaz begat Obed of Ruth; and Obed begat Jesse; and Jesse begat David the King; and David the King begat Solomon of her that had been the wife of Urias (Bethsheba); and Solomon begat Roboam; and Roboam begat Abia; and Abia begat Asa; and Asa begat*

Josaphat; and Josaphat begat Joram; and Joram begat Ozias; and Ozias begat Joatham; and Joatham begat Achaz; and Achaz begat Ezekias; and Ezekias begat Manasses; and Manasses begat Amon; and Amon begat Josias; and Josias begat Jechonias and his brethren, about the time they were carried away to Babylon; and after they were brought to Babylon, Jechonias begat Salathiel; and Salathiel begat Zorobabel; and Zorobabel begat Abiud; and Abiud begat Eliakim; and Eliakim begat Azor; and Azor begat Sadoc; and Sadoc begat Achim; and Achim begat Eliud; and Eliud begat Eleazar; and Eleazar begat Matthan; and Matthan begat Jacob; and Jacob begat Joseph, the husband of Mary of whom was born Jesus, who is called Christ. [1]

The birth of Jesus was the source of much speculation, surprise, and controversy among first century Hebrews—and the debate continues to the present day. The birth of Jesus Christ was prophesied in Isaiah. The Bible also describes in Matthew how it was possible for Mary to have a baby without being touched by a man:

Now the birth of Jesus Christ was on this wise: When as his mother, Mary was espoused to Joseph, before they came together, she was found with child of the Holy Ghost. [2]

Joseph was told by an angel of God that Mary was a virgin and to marry her.

Behold, a virgin shall be with child, and shall bring forth a son and they shall call his name Emmanuel, which means 'God with us.' [3]

Joseph knew Mary only after she had brought forth her firstborn son and called his name Jesus. Now when Jesus was born in Bethlehem of Judea in the days of Herod the King, behold, there came wise men from the east to Jerusalem. Saying where is he that is born King of the Jews? For we have seen his star in the East, and are come to worship him. When Herod the king had heard these things, he was troubled, and all Jerusalem with him. [4]

The three Wise men praised and worshipped the child, and gave him gifts. The Wise men departed a different way, and did not tell King

Herod what they saw. Later, an angel of the Lord appeared to Joseph in a dream and told him to flee with his family into Egypt. After the death of Herod, an angel again appeared and told Joseph to return with Mary and Jesus back to Israel.

> The Jewish historian and military leader in Galilee Flavius Josephus, who lived in the first century said, 'Jesus was a man of plain looks, extremely learned, and full of vigor, with dark skin.' [5]

It would seem that Jesus took on the looks of an everyday Israelite. He did not want to be treated differently because He came to serve and die for the sins of humankind. Both Daniel and John described the image of Jesus. Daniel wrote:

> *I beheld till the thrones were cast down, and the Ancient of days did sit, whose garment was white as snow, and the hair on his head like pure wool; his throne was like the fiery flame, and his wheels as burning fire.* [6]

The Original African Heritage Study Bible offers the following analysis of this verse:

> This prophecy revealed to Daniel, concerned the judgment of the Gentiles and establishment of an everlasting Kingdom of God. However, the King James Translators did not forget to use the word "Greece" which they referenced in Daniel's prophecy. Yet, these same translators saw "Sudanese" Africans in chains boarding ships, and they were being called Negroes! However, when these same Sudanese Kings sat on the thrones of Egypt, the translators then called them Ethiopians. [7]

John, in Revelation, sees similar physical features in the Messianic figure now called the Son of Man whose features are much like those previously noted in Daniel:

> *His head and his hairs were white like wool, as white as snow; and his eyes were as a flame of fire; His feet like unto fine brass, as if they burned in a furnace; and his voice as the sound of many waters.* [8]

8

This description seems to depict a person of color rather than a person of Caucasian descent. People of color were in the Bible; but it was hidden for centuries and their place in history was denied. The most important point of all of these, of course, is the identity of Jesus. Christians see Him as God incarnate, and the Savior of the world. Naturally, then, it is not surprising that different groups of people would want to claim Him as one of their own. There exists a vast amount of confusion that seemingly stems from deliberate European attempts to conceal the ethnic identity of some of the people of the Bible. When missionaries first went into Africa, they brought the Bible and the gun. When they left, they had gold and diamonds, and Africans had the Bible. But some of these missionaries were not spreading the true Gospel at all. Some had a completely non-Christian concept of African people. Some of the worst of them actually believed that Africans were without souls and were heathens. Did they believe that God only cared for Europeans? This reflected an extremely racist ideology on the part of some European Christians; a world view that prevailed for numerous centuries—maybe even to this present day.

The Introduction to *The Original African Heritage Study Bible* states:

> The origin of this people has been shrouded in the mysteries of the various versions and translations of the Bible (especially The King James version) for many years this was due, in part, to the misinterpretations of those who rendered the original translations from Hebrew and Greek into Latin, English, and other languages. However, a large portion of the confusion stems from the deliberate Euro centric attempts to conceal what today would be called the racial and/or ethnic identity of people of color in the Bible. [9]

Interestingly, very few translators bothered to translate the Holy Bible into the language that Jesus spoke—which was Aramaic. The Introduction continues:

In the name of religion, grave injustices have been perpetuated upon the entire world. These injustices have caused insurmountable suffering and pain. It is the collective consensus of the translators and their interpretations of this version of the Bible that the cycle of darkness must be broken, for the truth is the light, and with the truth all captives shall be set free. [10]

The Introduction concludes that:

The Bible is multicultural and multiracial with its purpose of being a universalism of the salvation story. Europeans are in the Bible. So are Asians and others. For example, in the New Testament the apostle Paul clearly intends to travel to Spain (Romans 15:24, 28). Also significantly included are Blacks and descriptions of Africa. [11]

The concept of inclusion is very important—the Bible itself is very inclusive—people from other lands are written about and people from various backgrounds are given credence for being "adopted" into the family of God. For example, the Ethiopian Eunuch of great authority under Candace queen of the Ethiopians, who had the charge of all her treasure, had come to Jerusalem to worship. Paraphrased from the book of Acts:

Phillip listened to what the angel of the Lord said to him, saying arise, and go toward the south unto the way that goeth down from Jerusalem unto Gaza. Phillip saw an Ethiopian reading Isaiah from pages of the Bible. And asked him if he understood what he was reading, and he said he needed someone to help him to understand. Phillip told him the meanings of the scriptures and he wanted to be baptized, Phillip baptized him. The Spirit of the Lord caught Phillip away. And the Eunuch went away rejoicing!

The following story is paraphrased from the book of John: Jesus needed to go to Samaria, which is called Sychar, near the plot of ground that Jacob gave to his son Joseph. A Samaritan woman came about noon to draw water from Jacob's well, this is when Jesus spoke to a Samaritan woman at the well and asked her for a drink of water. This was not the custom as Samaritans were considered to be inferior to the Jews, and they had no dealings with one another. Jesus told her to go and get her husband, and she answered and said I do not have a husband. Jesus told her, "you spoke truthfully you have had five husbands and the one you have now is not your own."

It is worth noting that this unnamed woman was the very first evangelist as she ran and told the men what Jesus had told her:

...and the men followed her back to where Jesus was at the well. Jesus told them about the living water as he had told the woman, and they believed.

Moving ahead in time; it seemed that Africa was known to most of the world. Also from *The Original African Heritage Study Bible:*

England was very familiar with the black man of Africa during the seventeenth century. The Muslims had long since given Africa the name "El Bilad es Sudan," translated "Land of the Blacks" or "the Black man's Land." England knew well that during the early days of the Old Testament Africa was called "The Land of Ham." England had entered the slave trade as early as 1552; Queen Elizabeth had money invested in the slave trade and in the colonies of the Americas to where the slaves were going. When the King James translators completed the translation in 1611, the black presence had long been a part of the English colony scenario. But the translators called them 'Negroes' instead of Ethiopians; hoping that the common minds of that day would see only color. [12]

One might conclude that had Africans been called by their proper title of Ethiopians it might have made a difference as to how the slave trade was conducted. Perhaps the money to be made from the trade of human cargo blinded most people of that day. Remember that all people are descended from Noah after the flood no matter how they look outwardly. Egyptians appear to have been looked upon as Black Africans by the other people of the then known world.

In the fifth century B.C. the Greek historian Herodotus referred to the Egyptians as being "black skinned with woolly hair."

> Even the term "Cush" which is used in the original Hebrew tongue (Kushites), was not employed. The translators knew by calling the slaves Negroes this would give no bearing to the White Christan world that the people they were enslaving were Christians well before Europe knew about the Risen Christ. [13]

> The Old Testament infers that the (Israelites) Jews considered the Egyptians to be a Black people. In chapter ten of Genesis all the "races" of the world are described as having been derived from Noah. [14]

According to James W. Peebles (one of ten contributors to *The Original African Heritage Study Bible*):

> Probably the greatest act that crystallized the justification of European slave trading was the Catholic priest Bartholomo de las Casas' writing in his encyclical to the papacy that these people (the Africans) were without souls and suitable for the torturous work in the Americas. [15]

De la Casa was not the only leader who felt as he did. Others too saw Africans as heathens without souls. God's prophesy upon Israel to 'bring thee into Egypt again with ships' was fulfilled:

> Over 100 million people were either taken captive or killed in the slave wars. About one-third of the Africans taken from their homes died on the way to the coast and at the embarkation stations, and another third died at sea, so that only one-third finally survived to become the laborers in the New World. [16]

One of the authors from the *OAHSB* describes how millions of Africans were taken from Africa:

> *And the Lord shall bring thee into Egypt again with ships, by the way whereof I spake unto thee, Thou shalt see it no more again: and there ye shall be sold unto your enemies for bondmen and bondwomen, and no man shall buy you.* [17]

In other words no man could keep them from being sent into slavery. It was God's method of making sure that the slavery in Egypt would be avenged. Remember God is no respecter of persons and since his chosen people, the Israelites, were disobedient to His laws, they were made to be slaves in Egypt for 430 years. Africans were also disobedient to God's law. Once taken into slavery men auctioned the slaves off to the highest bidder. One of the largest auction blocks was located in Washington, D.C. near where the White House is located today.

There are plenty of materials that prove the heritage of Jesus. In recent years in America there has been a proliferation of books and pamphlets representing a resurgence of what may be called an Afrocentric approach to the Bible. During the Biblical era in history, race or ethnicity did not matter in the way it seems to matter today. There was some ethnic (racial) disharmony between groups, for instance, the Jews and the Samaritans. However, in modern American society, anyone with a minuscule amount of African ancestry was/is considered Black. Accordingly, this would include Jesus and His mother, Mary, who had numerous people of color within their bloodlines. Paul declared in Galatians:

> There is neither Jew nor Greek, there is neither bond nor free, there is neither male nor female; for ye are all one in Christ Jesus. [18]

Paul could also have added there are neither black, white, brown, yellow, nor red people. The mere fact that he did not mention color is an indication that color had no importance at that time. Here is a summary of Sarah and Hagar:

> Abraham's wife Sarai had a handmaid, Hagar, who was an African woman given to Abraham in order that his wife might have children. At Sarai's directive Abram and Hagar the Egyptian brought forth Ishmael. This interrelationship joined together the two great African people of Shem and Ham, placing Abram as the father of both the Israelite (Jew) and Ishmaelite (Arab) nations. [19]

The problems continue until this present day— the hatred, fighting and distrust are a result of Sarai not waiting upon the Lord to have her own child. God did honor this word to Abram and to Sarai and she conceived and bore Isaac. Christians especially, we need to hear from God prior to doing anything. No matter how small or how large a situation God is still in control of everything and we must learn to trust Him for our lives. God also changed their names from Sarai to Sarah, and Abram to Abraham. This further shows that even people who are related can hate each other, because sin is the main culprit. And this is still the culprit in so-called 'race relations' in America today.

> Some of the information in this Bible which brings out truth and justice was not written by people of color. Today there are many Christians of Euro-gentile descent that are speaking out for God and His Divine Plan for the Black race. It is a fact to be considered that had it not been for secular historians both ancient and modern, there would have been little known about the peoples of Africa save the little that is hidden with the authorized King James version of the Bible. For some reason or another, religious writers, educators, and historians chose not to record the deeds of those from ancient Africa—the first land mass mentioned in the Bible. For the little information documented and known, Blacks and historians throughout the world have Arab travelers to thank for preserving the history of African kingdoms. Without their fair reports on the African civilizations during the Middle Ages and without work by Arab historians like Abderrahman, there would be no resources to shed light upon this important period in Africa's past. [20]

People of Color in the Bible

(Taken from *The Original African Heritage Study Bible*)

The Queen of Sheba

Sheba is an area at the southern tip of the Arabian Peninsula. Born to the family line of Shem and Ham, this queen was a descendant of Abraham and Keturah. She was also queen of a province called Sheba in Ethiopia. Praised for her beauty and wealth she earned international acclaim.

> *...tell of her visit to King Solomon where she marveled at the wisdom of his response to her many questions. King Solomon and the Queen of Sheba exchanged many gifts of great value and importance; she even bore him a son, Menelik I.*

Zipporah

Zipporah is identified as Moses' Cushite wife. It is said that Moses' brother Aaron and his sister Miriam did not like her. Some said this was because of the religion Zipporah believed in. According to *The Original African Heritage Study Bible,* there were others who claimed it was because Zipporah, Jethro's daughter, was a Black woman. The *OAHSB* also puts forward that Moses was an African Hebrew.

> *And Miriam and Aaron spoke against Moses because of the Ethiopian women who he had married, for he had married an Ethiopian woman.*

The Bible does state that her ethnicity (or color) was associated with the displeasure Aaron and Miriam expressed. Miriam seemingly had more negative words to say against Zipporah and God let His wrath be shown to her.

> *So the anger of the Lord was aroused against them, and He departed. And when the cloud departed from above the Tabernacle,*

suddenly Miriam became leprous, as white as snow. Then Aaron turned towards Miriam, and there she as a leper.

Aaron went to Moses, and asked his brother to save Miriam from this horrible disease. Moses implored the Lord God for mercy, and was told Miriam would have to suffer for seven days in isolation before re-appearing in a healed state. This curse came from God, not man.

Ebedmelech

This Ethiopian eunuch saved the life of the prophet Jeremiah. He saw the miserable fate of Jeremiah, who had been thrown into the dungeon where he sunk into the mire.

Concerned Jeremiah would die in these conditions, Ebedmelech reported to King Zedekiah, asking if they might not remove Jeremiah from this desperate situation. The King allowed this rescue, and sent Ebedmelech to rescue Jeremiah from the dungeon. Still in prison but in more satisfactory conditions, Jeremiah was then able to plead his case to the King, and was eventually freed.

Hagar

Hagar was the Egyptian handmaiden of Abraham's wife, Sarah, who was barren. Sarah offered Hagar to satisfy Abraham, who desired a son. Hagar bore Abraham a son, Ishmael; making the Arabs first cousins to the Israelites.

Tirhakah

A king of Ethiopia and Egypt in the twenty-fifth dynasty, Tirhakah was an opponent to the Assyrian king for the domination of Palestine. He attempted to defend Egypt against the Assyrian king, but was defeated in the delta and driven south into Upper Egypt, where he maintained a rule of some dignity at Thebes.

And he heard say concerning Tirhakah, King of Ethiopia, he is come forth to make war with thee, and when he heard it, he sent messengers to Hezekiah, saying, Thus shall ye speak to Hezekiah, King of Juda, saying let not the God, in whom you trusted deceive thee, saying, Jerusalem shall not be delivered into the hand of the king of Assyria."

Asenath

Asenath was the Egyptian wife of Joseph, son of Jacob (renamed Israel), given to him by the Pharaoh. Asenath and Joseph had two sons, Manasseh and Ephraim.

And Pharaoh called Joseph's name Zaph'-nath-pa-a-a-new; and he gave him a wife, As'e-nath, the daughter of Pot-I-ph'-rah, priest of On. And Joseph went out over all the land of Egypt.

Simon of Cyrene

Simon was ordered to help Jesus to carry the cross, and Cyrene was an ancient city in Libya, an African country.

And they compelled one Simon, a Cy-re'-ni-an, who passed by, coming out of the country, the father of Alexander and Rufus, to help Jesus to bear his cross.

Controversy rages over the color of numerous others such as King Solomon. Reading the Songs of Solomon, the king's lyrical prose, some conclude he too was a Black man. Solomon's song-like book was devoted to his relationship with Makeda, better known as the Queen of Sheba.

There are many passages that speak to people of color in the Bible, especially when areas such as Egypt and Ethiopia are mentioned. In the Bible, Egypt is mentioned 155 times and Ethiopia is mentioned 45 times. If people and places were not important then God would not have included them in His holy book. Moses was a man of color; if he had not been, then the following from Exodus could not have taken place:

And the Lord furthermore said unto him, put now thine hand into thy bosom. And he put his hand into his bosom: and when he took it out, behold, his hand was leprous as snow...And he said, put thine hand into thy bosom again. And he put his hand into his bosom again; and plucked it out of his bosom, and, behold, it was turned again as his other flesh.

Moses, a Hebrew, was born in Egypt and was also a descendant of Abraham. While engaging in dialogue with God, Moses was shown an outstanding sign of God's power; by placing his hand on his bosom it became "leprous as snow." The predominant and characteristic form of leprosy in the Old Testament was of a white variety, covering the entire body or a large part of its surface. This act of turning "tanned" flesh white and then back again was truly a miracle. If people's skin had originally been white in color, the color would have remained the same or somewhat similar, however it came as an amazement to Moses to see the difference in his skin tone. Leprosy was a sickness and it was deadly in many cases.

Author's Note: It is my contention that a mild case would render the people light, pale, or "whitish" similar to being an albino without color. These people would group together and move away from the pigmented others, which would lead towards another group of people with a fair complexion. It depended on the location of where they lived whether they remained "light," or not.

And I had made of one blood all nations of men for to dwell on all the face of the earth, and hath determined the times before appointed, and the bounds of their habitation
(Acts 17:26)

Chapter III.

Civilization in Africa

Civilization started in the great river valleys of Africa and the Middle East, and in the fertile crescent along the Nile River. Interestingly, the Greeks included a few tidbits on Africans in their records, but they could have done far more to shed light on this "dark continent." According to George G.M. James in his book *Stolen Legacy,* "Greek philosophy is stolen Egyptian philosophy." The Greeks, like some other Europeans, stole, lied, and claimed credit that they did not deserve. They coveted the honor of transmitting to the world the Arts, Sciences and other inventions that had originated in Africa. The many firsts and significant contributions made to the world by Africans were simply appropriated by them in the process of record keeping. On this subject I would recommend the excellent film by Dr. William Cosby whose documentary *Lost, Strayed or Stolen,* provides information about Black History many years ago. Also, According to Lerone Bennett, Jr. in his book Before the Mayflower:

> When the human drama opened, Africans were on the scene and acting. For a long time, in fact, the only people on the scene were Africans. For some 600,000 years, Africa and Africans led the world. Were these people who gave the world fire and tools, and cultivated grain—were they Negroes? [1]

The origins of humankind are found in the Ancient Land of Judah-Kush (Ethiopia), the Garden of Eden in the Bible (Genesis 2:13), which is referred to summarily in ancient text as "The Land of the Gods" and "The Heartland of African Civilization." At one time in remote antiquity, the ancient land known today as Ethiopia included all the land known as Africa, including parts of Asia (Kindu-Kush), and the Middle East (Yemen, Israel and Palestine). The southern portion of the Atlantic was known as the Ethiopian Ocean. Bennett continues:

> In the Nile Valley, that beginning was an African as well as an Asian achievement. Negroes, or people who would be considered Negroes today, were among the first people to use tools, paint pictures, plant seeds and worship gods. Back there, in the beginning, blackness was not an occasion for obloquy. In fact, the reverse seems to have been true. White men were sometimes ridiculed for the "unnatural whiteness of their skin. [2]

Lerone Bennett, Jr. often stated that slavery was not new, it was as old as the Bible. It seems that most of the people in ancient times were people of color; honored and known throughout the ancient world. Bennett continues:

> Slavery, in one form or another, has been practiced in every country known to man. Slavery was old when Moses was young. In Plato's Athens and Caesar's Rome, men—white, black, and brown—were bought and sold. Slavery existed in the Middle Ages in Christian Europe and in so-called "pagan" Africa. [3]

Bennett says that men from all backgrounds have been enslaved at some time in history. Color has intentionally been the primary focus for abuse from some Europeans towards Africans; yet early traders and foreigners did not seem to mind trading with Africans. The distinction between one skin color and another was not significant during this period in history. The skin tone of a person did not indicate one's race or ethnic origin, instead the clothing that one wore spoke to the status one held and seemed of primary importance. Europeans used religion to justify their exploitation of people of color, including Africans and Native Americans. Europeans felt it necessary to "save the heathens" by introducing them to Christianity. Africans already knew God, and they were great entrepreneurs of that day. Africans led the way for trading in the known world, and they were treated as equals prior to the time of Columbus. Bennett continues:

> Some of the African countries especially in north Africa and Ethiopia had a form of written language, with pictograms and other ideograms using basic drawings and symbols to communicate, but none were more advanced than Egypt. Egyptians used the written symbols of their day to write on papyrus, wood and stone. The early carvings date back to 196 B.C. where they used logographic and alphabetic symbols in their writings. The Egyptians used cursive hieroglyphs for religious entries on papyrus, wood or stone (the Rosetta Stone was found in Egypt by the French in 1799). They used demotic script which was common, and they later wrote in Greek which was the language of the rulers of Egypt at that time. The fact is that it could reasonably be argued that writing itself is an African invention! [4]

However, some African countries used the oral method of communicating. Their history and important knowledge concerning the tribes was passed on by mouth from one generation to the next. The Greeks wrote their history and included some Africans in their recordings. Bennett includes some better-known classical Greek writers:

> Homer, Herodotus, Pliny, Diodorus, and other classical writers repeatedly praised the Ethiopians. "The annals of the great early nations of Asia Minor are full of them," Lady Flora Louisa Lugard writes. "The mosaic records allude to them frequently; but while they are described as the most powerful, the most just, and the most beautiful of the human race, they are constantly spoken of as black, and there seems to be no other conclusion to be drawn, than that at that remote period of history the leading race of the Western World was a black race." [5]

Greeks knew that the African race were the (most) powerful, just, and beautiful of all the races. This was a very honest description of Africans at that time in history. Some of my latest research has taken me to a book by George G.M. James. *Stolen Legacy* (which I mentioned before), describes the reasons that Greeks knew so much philosophy—they stole it from Egypt! James states:

> The true authors of Greek philosophy were not the Greeks; but the people of North Africa, commonly called Egyptians; and the praise and honor falsely given to the Greeks for centuries belong to people of North Africa, and therefore to the African Continent. Consequently this theft of the African legacy by the Greeks has led to the erroneous world opinion that the African Continent had made no contribution to civilization. And that its people are naturally backward. This is the misrepresentation that has become the basis of racial prejudice, which has affected all people of color. [6]

Research is very important when writing on various subjects. There is always information that one might not have previously known. Are the history book going to be rewritten? This author doubts it, but this is important knowledge that needs to be known by the world.

Africans were pioneers in developing and inventing tools, and other implements that benefited the world. Franz Boas writes from Rogers:

> It seems likely that at a time when the European was still satisfied with crude stone tools, the African had invented and adopted the art of smelting iron. Consider for a moment what this had meant for the advance of the human race… A great progress was made when copper found in large nuggets was hammered out into tools and later on shaped by smelting, and when bronze was introduced many items were made; however, but the true advancement of industrial life did not begin until the hard iron was discovered. It seems not unlikely that the people who made the marvelous discovery of reducing iron ore smelting were the African Negroes. Neither ancient Europe nor western Asia nor ancient China knew iron, and everything points to its introduction from Africa. [7]

At the time of the great African discoveries the trade of blacksmithing was found all over Africa, from north to south, and from east to west. With their simple bellows and a charcoal fire, they reduced the ore that was found in many parts of the continent and forged implements of great usefulness and beauty. The world has Africa to thank for the many inventions and advancements that helped all of mankind! Iron smelting and other items needed for mankind to survive were discoveries made in Africa; for it seems that the only people doing anything at that time in history were Africans. Again, it seems only until recent times has most of this factual information emerged in many old and some recent books. Very few African contributions were properly recorded.

Joel Augustus Rogers, Lerone Bennet, Ivan Van Sertima, Dr. Leo Wiener, and Dr's. L.S.B. & Mary Leakey's discoveries have however led the way to uncovering the truth about Africa, and its people. Many of the written contributions about Africans were written by persons from multicultural and multi-ethnic groups. To this day Leakey's findings have not been disproved. According to J. A. Rogers:

> In that portion of the globe to which the stalwart Anglo-Saxon Stanley gave the name of 'dark' and 'darkest.' The light upon the people of that continent whose children we are accustomed to regard as types of natural servility with no recorded history. But the spell has been broken. The buried treasure of antiquity again revisits the sun. He gave abundant proof of rich archaeological and other finds, which since have been supplemented by the Mond Expedition in Sudan; the researches of Professor L.S.B. Leakey in East Africa; and Professors Broom and Dart in South Africa. Leakey discovered remains of the Boskop Man, a bushman type of some 30,000 years ago; and Broom and Dart types that go still farther back. Their researches appear to bear out what an earlier anthropologist, Prichard, said in his "Physical History of Man." Namely, "The primitive stock of men were probably Negroes and I know of no argument to be set on the other side. Europe itself when it was still joined to Africa was tropical and was inhabited by Negroes." [8]

As previously mentioned above, James Cowles Prichard, in 1813, in his book (referenced above) defends the biblically based argument that all mankind was of one species. He advanced an interesting hypothesis concerning the processes of racial differentiation, and suggested the then daring possibility that original men were black-skinned[1]*. Note: the period was too far out. Interestingly enough, Prichard's goal was to trace to a single source for all the races of man from the earliest historical records to the dispersion of mankind after the Deluge.

After the flood, the Noah's Ark episode, Noah and his family were the only humans left to populate the earth. The abundant artifacts and documented materials warrant acceptance of Africa as the birthplace of all of humanity. According to Gerald Horne:

> The human race probably developed in Asia or Africa. Modern people were present in Europe 50,000 years ago, and they may have been there 5,000 years before that. It is now believed that the first human beings reached America possibly more than 15,000 years ago. There is a general agreement that they came via the Bering Strait to populate the Western hemisphere name-ly North America and South America. [9]

According to many historians, archaeologists, and researchers, such as Leakey, Rogers, Van Sertima, Wiener and Bennett, whom all studied Africans and their contributions, Africa was and is the "Cradle of Civilization." African people were the first to use tools, paint pic-tures, and plant seeds. According to Berkin, et al:

> Some 1,000,000 years ago, humans began to spread out from the grasslands of Africa, traveling by way of Asia. Passing through Siberia these people reached the land bridge and crossed over populating the Western Hemisphere some time later. The people came, anthropologists believe, between 12,000 and 30,000 years ago during the last Ice Age, a time when much of the Earth's water was frozen in huge glaciers. The crossing was called the 'land bridge'— where the Bering Strait now flows, (it is speculated that the land bridge fell away and is now under the

---

*   Prichard was one of the "fathers" of Anthropology.

Bering Strait). Theorists think that the hunter-gatherers were following the giant mammoths and mastodons, trying to keep up with their food supply. [10]

A number of scientists and scholars both in ancient and modern times, have concluded that the world's first civilization was the creation of a people now known as Ethiopians. Much of the recent information that has been "unearthed" came about because of the willingness of some Greeks and Arabs who wrote about the African contribution to civilization. A few Greeks also wrote about how they borrowed ('stole', according to James) scientific, legal, medical, and mathematical information from Africans. It was they who named the land Ethiopia; after the word the Hellenes used when they first came into contact with the dark inhabitants of Africa; meaning "burnt faces."

Most World History books attribute all of the above-mentioned contributions to Greeks. It is well recorded and heralded that Greece led the way to modern civilization, but less well known that they borrowed their contributions from their associates and traders in Africa. Nevertheless, if Africans were mentioned, evidently many of their discoveries were left out of the books. Bennett states that many European traders found Africans to be equals in trade and commerce, where both Europeans and Africans benefited. Bennett writes:

> The Ethiopians claimed to be the spiritual fathers of Egyptian civilization. Diodorus Siculus, the Greek historian who wrote in the first century B.C., said: "The Ethiopians conceived themselves to be of greater antiquity than any other nation; and it is probable that, born under the sun's path, its warmth may have ripened them earlier than other men. They supposed themselves to be the inventors of worship, of festivals, of solemn assemblies, of sacrifices, and every religious practice." [11]

Ethiopia is a very ancient nation; no doubt they were among the earliest humans to make discoveries that others have relied on throughout history. Seeing the sights of a developing Ethiopia would have been be very impressive to anyone when most other places were still crude in development. Historically speaking, many Europeans were often sold into slavery earlier in history. Somehow humans tend to continue the cycle of violence and inhumane treatment towards fellow humans. Bennett further states:

> How did the Egyptians see themselves? They painted themselves in three colors: black, reddish-brown, yellow. The color white was available to them, but they used it to portray blue-eyed, white-skinned foreigners. One of the great murals of Egyptian art is the procession from a tomb of Thebes in the time of Thotmes III. The Egyptians and Ethiopians in the procession are painted in the usual brown and black colors. Thirty-seven whites in the procession are rendered in white tones. Who were they? G.A. Hoskins said they were probably "white slaves of the king of Ethiopia sent to the Egyptian king as the most acceptable present." [12]

Amazingly enough Egyptians did not regard themselves as being "White." Far from it they seemed content to portray themselves with darker hues in their self-portraits. Rogers wrote:

> In regards to the title, *"Africa's Gift to America"*, it is fitting to recall that Africa played a role, perhaps the chief role, in the earliest development of America—a period that antedates Columbus by many centuries, namely Aztec, Maya and Inca Civilizations. About 500 A.D. or earlier, Africans sailed over to the Americas and continued to do so until the time of Columbus. This does not call for any particular stretch of the imagination. Africa is only 1600 miles distant from South America with islands in between, among them are St. Paul and Fernando Noronha. [13]

The Islands in the Atlantic Ocean provided a place for Africans coming to the New World. There were fruits and fish to eat and the island natives were receptive (this of course was prior to the conquest of Columbus, and other European explorers who made no exception concerning the status of Africans; all were treated cruelly).

In Jackson's book *God, Man, and Civilization,* he included an article Davidson wrote for the magazine West Africa in 1969. Jackson wrote concerning Basil Davidson:

> Africans Before Columbus. He wrote Columbus and other early European arrivals in America came back with quite a bit of evidence, suggestive but inclusive, that black peoples from Africa had already reached those shores. Various writers have pointed from time to time, over the past twenty years and more, to the likely West African origins of these black explorers, notably of that tribe of Almamys who were said to have settled in Honduras. [14]

According to Bennett slavery was a way of life. One could be a slave one day, and the next day he or she could become a great leader, as this form of slavery carried no negative connotations. According to Van Sertima from his book *They Came Before Columbus:*

> The Indians gave proof that they were trading with black people. They brought to the Spanish concrete evidence of this trade. The Indians claim that in Espanola there had come a black people who have the tops of their spears made of a metal which they call guanin, of which he (Columbus) had sent samples to the Sovereigns to have them assayed, when it was found that of parts, 18 were of gold, 6 of silver and 8 of copper. The origin of the word guanin may be traced down in the Mande languages of West Africa, through Mandingo, Kabunga, Toronka, Kankanka, Bambara, Mande and Vei. In Vei, we have the form of the word ka-ni which transliterated into native phonetics, would give us gua-nin. In Columbus's journal "gold" is given as coa-na, while guanin is recorded as an island where there is much gold. [15]

These metal components were from African tradition only. They can be found in the islands in the West Indies comprising of the Republic of Haiti and the Dominican Republic. The presence of Blacks with their trading mastery in America, before Columbus, is proven by the representation of Blacks in Native American sculpture and design. Rogers stated:

> As late as 1650 the South Atlantic was called the Ethiopic, or Ethiopian Ocean, and most of Africa as far as South Africa was called Ethiopia. [16]

The landmasses might have been closer because the land was joined together in many places where it is no longer joined. The countries were larger landmasses as well. It is not impossible for Africans to be on the various islands or other extended places. (Hispanola), or Espanola were the islands of Haiti and Santa Domingo. Interestingly, enough Dr. Wiener's book *Africans and the Discovery of America,* agrees with Van Sertima. Rogers on Dr. Wiener:

> Professor Wiener found that these Negro traders traveled as far north as New England. Their relics have been found in graves there, most notably a pipe with Negro face. [17]

Other writers have alluded to the fact that guanin, a metal from Africa, was found in the New World, proving that Africans brought these metals with them. The presence of Negro traders from Guinea, who trafficked in a gold alloy, guanin; of precisely the same composition and bearing the same name, was frequently referred to by other early writers on Africa. Rogers notes:

> In the fifteenth Century, we find other periodic influxes of Africans in Europe that began under the Pharaohs. They came this time not as conquerors, like the Moors, but as slaves; principally in Portugal and Spain and as far north as England, around 1440 or 1442, some 50 years before the discovery of the New World. Having proved so useful, it was inevitable that the Spaniards would bring them to the New World. [18]

Dr. Leo Wiener began his research in the early 1920s. Although Africans were later reintroduced to America in slavery, they had preceded Europeans by many hundreds of years. Dr. Wiener's extraordinary research came in the form of a three-volume set of books entitled *Africa and the Discovery of America.* Bennett writes:

As political entities, Ghana, Mali and Songhay do not suffer in comparison with their European contemporaries. In several areas, in fact, the Sudanese empires were clearly superior. "It would be interesting to know," what the Normans might have thought of Ghana. Anglo-Saxon England could easily have seemed a poor and lowly place beside it. [19]

It seems that Africa was far more advanced compared to other known worlds. This high civilization was well noted by the Greeks, and because of them we now know of their accomplishments. Africans were travelers, traders and well-established businessmen, long before the European invasion. Rogers writes about Count Volney:

> Two thousand years later another famous traveler, Count Volney, said on his visit to Egypt in 1787, that what Herodotus said had solved for him the problem of why the people were so Negroid in appearance and especially the Great Sphinx of Ghizeh, supreme symbol of worship and power. Reflecting on the then state of the Egyptians compared with what they had been, he said, to think that a race of black men who are today our slaves and the object of our contempt is the same one to whom we owe our arts, sciences and even the very use of speech. [20]

Amazingly some of the civil and religious systems that still govern the United States of America and other first world nations came from the Black group. Rogers continues with his research on Count Volney:

> Count Volney continues: Of the blacks he saw in Upper Egypt among the ruins of the colossal monuments there, he said, there a people now forgotten discovered while others were yet barbarians, the elements of the arts and science. A race of men now rejected from society for their sable skin and woolly hair, founded on the study of the laws of nature those civil and religious systems which still govern the universe. [21]

It seems clear that for hundreds or perhaps thousands of years Africans and their contributions were deleted from the annals of the world's history books. Rogers notes that J.G. Jackson wrote in 1809:

> They, (the Moors) carried the Christian captives (mainly whites) about the desert to the different markets to sell them but they soon discovered that their habits of life render them unserviceable, or very inferior to the black slaves from Timbuctoo. After traveling three days to one market, five to another, nay, sometimes fourteen, they at length become objects of commercial speculation and the itinerant Jew traders, who wander about Wedinoon to sell their wares find means to barter them for tobacco, salt, a cloth garment, or any other thing. [22]

Historically speaking, Europeans as well as Africans were sold into slavery at an early time in history. This author has a very hard time understanding the mindset of people, once humiliated themselves and down trodden, would do such mean and unseemly things to others. Africans were the victims of a maniacal scheming of a contemptuous group of angry people getting their revenge for the mistreatment they suffered for a period of time in ancient history. Bennett states that men from all backgrounds have been enslaved at some point in history. Color has intentionally been the primary focus for abuse from Europeans, and their hatred of the Africans. Early traders and foreigners did not seem to be troubled by trading with Africans. The distinction between one skin color and another was not significant. The skin tone of a person did not indicate one's race or ethnic origin. Africans and Native Americans especially have been mistreated because of their 'color.' Europeans felt it necessary to "save the heathens" by introducing them to Christianity. However, much of Africa had already known Christianity; especially because the first man made in God's own image existed very near to, or inside, Africa itself.

Africans led the way for world trading and were treated as equals or, should it be said, they were treated as kings and dignitaries prior to the conquest of Columbus. In fact, Rogers says that Columbus received information about the Americas from Africans in Spain and Portugal prior to his "discovery" of America. They reported that riches and wonderful things were to be found in Espanola. According to Rogers, Dr. Wiener concludes:

In Africa and the Discovery of America, he gives abundant proof that they were. He says, "The presence of Negroes before Columbus is proved by the representation of Negroes in American sculpture and design; by the occurrence of a black nation at Darien* early in the 16th Century and more specifically by Columbus' empathic reference to Negro traders from Guinea (Ghana), who trafficked in gold alloy of precisely the same composition and bearing the same name (Guanin), is frequently referred to by early writers on Africa. [23]

*Darien is an arm of the Caribbean between NE Panama and NW Columbia. It is the former name for the Isthmus of Panama. Actually Africans were then reintroduced to America in slavery. Many hundreds or thousands of years prior, Africans had been in the Western Hemisphere.

The presence of Blacks, with all their trading mastery in America, before Columbus, is proven by the representation of Blacks in Native American sculpture and design. Rogers states that Columbus received information from Africans that were in Spain and Portugal prior to his "discovery" of America. Rogers states:

C.C. Marquez says, "The Negro type is seen in the most ancient Mexican sculpture… Negroes figure frequently in the most remote tradition." Riva Palacio, a Mexican historian says "it is indisputable that in very ancient times the Negro race occupied our territory (Mexico) when the two continents were joined. The Mexicans recall a Negro god, Ixilton, which had a man's 'black face' [24]

Please take another look at the cover of this book, the face is that of the Black faced god Ixilton from Mexico. Continuing with Rogers concerning N. Leon:

The almost extinction of the original Negroes during the time of the Spanish conquest and the memories of them in the most ancient traditions induce us to believe that the Negroes were the first inhabitants of Mexico. [25]

The Olmecs (an early people) from Mexico worshipped a god they called Ixilton, which was a black-faced gigantic head with African features and tight curled hair. The people were dark that inhabited Mexico in ancient history. This is in agreement with Van Sertima's book *They Came Before Columbus*. Old maps were hugely beneficial in providing the names of the oceans and certain locations at an earlier time in history.

However, then Whites had no conception of being white, or its so-called importance. Research has shown that in earlier periods in history Whites did not seem to think very much of their skin color. The majority of people with whom they dealt were persons of color, and it did not seem to matter.

Legal documents from the time identified Whites as Englishmen or Christians. The word "white," with its burden of arrogance and biological pride, developed late in the century as a direct result of European instigation. Historically, the word "white" was used for the most part in reference to clothing or other items surrounding a person, not the color of skin. Van Sertima continues:

> The truth is "white" is a purely European convention when used as an exclusive reference for skin color and race, "White" in American Indian terms did not mean (in pre-Columbian times) Caucasian. Quetzalcoatl did not have Northern Europeans features. Native Americans spoke of him at times as being white in symbolic sense, in the way Muslims may speak of Mohammed as a handful of white light in Allah's palm. A black or brown Negroid Hamitic man, as Abubakari was, appearing out of the east in long flowing white Muslim robes would be called white. [26]

At this period in history "color" did not seem to have the same significance as in recent years. For example: Egyptians painted in their caves and made colored paintings, whenever people were depicted they were always other colors not "white." There are many speculations concerning this phenomenon, however, suffice it to say that somehow three-fourths of the world is of color and only one-fourth is considered to be Caucasian. Clothing sometimes represented whether a person belonged to one group or another. As the European developed skills for recording information it seems likely that they recorded history as if all discoveries came from them. As mentioned, it is noteworthy that Egyptians did not consider themselves as being "white" or light. They always saw themselves a color other than white. It is understandable that they were proud of their color, as they should have been.

Dr. Leo Wiener began his studies in the early 1900s. Although Africans were later re-introduced to America in slavery, they had preceded Europeans by many hundreds of years. Dr. Leo Wiener was treated very unfairly when he worked at Harvard University, mainly because he wrote about Africans having being in America prior to Columbus' arrival. And he was of European descent.

Needless to say bigotry and discrimination were alive and well during the 1920s while Dr. Wiener was at Harvard. Professor Wiener found that African traders traveled as far north into the Americas as New England. Their relics have been found in graves, such as "a pipe with a Negro face." These relics were undeniably African in origin. Dr. Wiener believed Africans had brought these relics when they crossed the ocean via a land bridge or boat. Africans were very talented and ingenious in that they were able to make things that caused many to wonder how it was possible.

Africans have never been given credit for many of their contributions to the world; nor were they given credit for their many inventions in America. Most people do not know of the contributions made during, after, and to this day by African Americans (this author lists just a few in the Conclusion).

Africans made large boats with many floors and elaborate trim, often in gold. Van Sertima states that Thor Heyerdahl believed the Africans were capable of making reed boats or rafts that could sail the Atlantic. Van Sertima explores how Thor Heyerdahl, a Norwegian ethnologist, author and explorer, actually set out to examine the claims of the rafts and small boats crossing the Atlantic Ocean. This gave the needed validity to claims that Africans had indeed traversed the oceans. From Heyerdahl's voyages. According to Van Sertima:

> With Buduma tribesmen under the direction of Abdullah Djibrine, a papyrus expert from Lake Chad, a replica of the ancient papyrus boat was built. Heyerdahl called this the Ra I, the word for sun in ancient Egypt as well as in parts of America and on all the islands of Polynesia. The Ra I set out from Safi, on the Atlantic coast of North Africa, on May 25, 1969. It sailed to within a few days of the New World before it got into serious trouble. The Heyerdahl expedition had made one mistake. In the Egyptian model a rope ran down from the curved tip of the stern to the afterdeck. It was thought that this rope was only there to maintain the curve of the stern. In fact, the stern, through this rope, acted as a spring supporting the pliant afterdeck. The ill-advised removal of this rope caused the afterdeck to sag, and the boat listed dangerously as it neared Barbados. [27]

This first voyage made the news and people were amazed that a raft could make such a long and difficult voyage. The fact that it only reached the islands did not seem to matter. Heyerdahl's exploits continue according to Van Sertima:

> A smaller model, Ra II, built on the identical Egyptian pattern by a Native American tribe, the Aymara, who profited from this trial and error, made it across the Atlantic from Africa as necessary. What Heyerdahl had proven, in effect, was the most ancient of Egyptian ships, predecessors of even more sophisticated models, could have crossed the Atlantic. He demonstrated also, through the shipbuilding labors of the Buduma tribesmen, that these navigational skills had been largely preserved among riverine and Lacustrine Africans even to the present day. The papyrus boat however is but a modest curtain raiser on the vast theater of ancient Egyptian shipping. [28]

Many issues arose due to the fact that the native's advice was not followed in the building of the RA I. However, they listened to the

Ayamaras when building the RA II and the journey was successful all the way into the Western Hemisphere.

Many people have speculated that Africans were "landlocked" and thus not able to navigate the waters that surrounded their continent (this author visited Africa and actually saw children swimming the Atlantic Ocean). Most Africans learn to swim in lakes, rivers and the ocean, and are magnificent swimmers. They learn to swim early as a matter of survival. Scholars have long speculated that a great seafaring nation once existed on Africa's west coast and they sent ships to the Americas. Many Europeans did not want to know about the early development in Egypt or any parts of Africa. Some Europeans made a concerted effort to erase these facts from the pages of history to keep them pristine and white at any cost. Africans gave the world marvelous inventions, many of which are still in present use. Africa has provided food and plants that are used in America even today. Africans have contributed to the world and to the Americas.

The presence of Africans was evident and preserved in Mexican records. This is true of Columbus. On his third voyage he stated that he saw Negroes.

When the years of the 1400s are taken into account the figure of over 430 years emerges for the New World slavery, almost identical to the length of time Israelites were under slavery in Egypt. Remember, Columbus was setting sail East for India therefore, when he arrived West instead of East the natives he encountered he called "Indians." Van Sertima continues:

> The African presence in America before Columbus is of importance not only to African and American history but also to the history of world civilizations. It provides further evidence that all great civilizations and races are heavily indebted to one another and that no race has a monopoly on enterprises and inventive genius. Stone heads prove the African presence; terra cottas, skeletons, artifacts, techniques and inscriptions. There is also proof of the African presence from oral tradition and

documented history, by botanical, linguistic and cultural data. When the feasibility of African crossings of the Atlantic was not proven and the archaeological evidence undated and unknown, we could in all innocence ignore the most startling of coincidences. This is no longer possible. The case for African contacts with pre-Columbian America, in spite of a number of understandable gaps and a few minor elements of contestable data, is no longer based on the fanciful conjecture and speculation of romantics. It is grounded now upon an overwhelming and growing body of reliable witnesses. Using Dr. Rhine's dictum or phenomena that were once questionable but are now being empirically confirmed, truly it may be said: The overwhelming incidence of coincidence argues overwhelmingly against a mere coincidence. [29]

This overview by Van Sertima sums up the materials that have been included in this chapter to show that many contributions and inventions were provided to the world by Africans.

The contributors to this area of study were themselves multicultural and came from diverse backgrounds. Being exposed to their research was in itself a great inspiration to write my book. There was/ is a preponderance of evidence that shows African Americans have indeed contributed to many inventions and ingenious devices made available to America. The New World had so many artifacts from Africa that it was very difficult to deny that they had arrived at such locations. It seems that men from various educational fields of study with substantial credentials now authenticate early expeditions by Africans. There are many myths surrounding Africa, this author has chosen a few:

- Africa nurtured a landlocked race of people
- Africa had no knowledge of lands not connected to her
- Africa never had any mariners
- Africa never constructed boats
- Africa's empires ended at the edge of the desert
- Africa is unwashed by the world's seas

These myths are found in history books as well as other historical sources, and this book has dismantled most of these myths. J.A. Rogers notes that "Africans were navigating the Atlantic before Christ."

Rogers and Wiener concur that Africans were a seafaring group. Interestingly enough, Dr. Leo Wiener's discoveries were never disproved, neither were Dr. L.S.B. Leakey's many findings, or Joel Augustus Rogers (he wrote over twelve books on Africans and African Americans); to date none have been disputed. Ivan Van Sertima's works are also held in high esteem. These are just a few of the many authors, historians, researchers, philologists, archeologists, ethnologist, educators and other scientific scholars who have contributed to making these important facts known. Africans have a place in history, as they have contributed to world civilizations as well as to American history. However, it was the Greeks who wrote a minuscule amount of information that gave Africans some contributions in antiquity. Africa is a very large continent with several countries mentioned dating back to Biblical days.

The African continent is made up of over 50 countries with people speaking over 2,500 languages and dialects; they also have different cultures and customs from one country to the other. Centuries of contact and interbreeding have already produced different looking Africans. Some West Africans are short and broad-nosed, some are tall with straight hair and aquiline noses. Africans are all colors: chocolate, asphalt, café au lait, persimmon, and cream. These definitions came from Lerone Bennett, Jr.—these descriptions are so nice, I wish I could have claimed them for myself.

Blacks, like any other people, look different from one another. Subtle to marked variations occur from region to region. But evidently, to some European scholars and slavers, there were no differences at all. Africans were all treated the same, no matter how important the roles of some of the African dignitaries might have been. The main characteristic apparent to some Europeans was their Black skin. The only "equality" these slavers practiced was a parity of bigotry and unbridled cruelty toward those they sought to subjugate, dehuman-ize, and treat like chattel property; this was the plight of the African when he was re-introduced to the Americas.

Judge not, that ye be not judged
(Matthew 7:1)

Chapter IV.

The Social Significance of Race and Ethnicity

Sociology is a relatively new science created in the nineteenth century with its roots steeped in European thought and behavior. The discipline proposes to be the scientific, empirical study of man's behavior in various groups and settings. This chapter will embrace "race and ethnicity" as it relates to sociology. Dr. John Macionis wrote great sociology textbooks and they were my preference to use in my sociology classes at the University of Alaska, in Anchorage, Alaska. Here are the sociological meanings of race and ethnicity from Dr. Macionis:

Race: is a category composed of men and women who share biologically transmitted traits that are defined as socially significant. Races are commonly distinguished by physical traits such as skin color, hair texture, shape of facial features, and body type. Racial diversity appeared among our human ancestors as the result of living in different geographical regions of the world. Members of a single biological species, human beings display biological variations—described as "racial characteristics" In regions of intense heat, for example, humans developed darker skin (from the natural pigment, melanin) as protection from the sun; in regions with moderate climates, people have lighter skin. Such differences are literally-only skin deep because every human being the world over is a member of a single biological species. [1]

According to Dr. Macionis, such differences are literally-only skin deep because every human being the world over is a member of a single biological species. This author agrees, that humans no matter what they look like on the outside are from a single biological species. Which means that all humans are basically the same. However, it seems that early in European history a mind-set of racial superiority evolved that permeated the entire world. One of the most fearsome examples of this would be Hitler's ideology of death and destruction towards anyone who wasn't Aryan during the era when his maniacal Nazi regime was in power in Germany. This was the beginning of modern "racism." The idea that one group of people was "superior" to another became a common practice, especially in America. Social scientists in Europe decided anthropology would be the "vehicle" that would place Europeans above all other groups. They made up the guidelines, naturally writing in favor of their features and characteristics.

This was the beginning of a systemic racism using the superiority complex of the Aryan group (that is blue eyes and blond hair). Sociologists of today, as a group, tend not to adhere to any such notions nor do they tend to give any platform for this line of reasoning. The distinctions and variations between human groups came about for many reasons, unrelated to the inferiority of some groups or the superiority of others. However, nineteenth century biologists studying the world's racial diversity developed a three-part typology. Also from Dr. Macionis:

> Man has made three classifications of humanity. The people with lighter skin and finer softer hair were called Caucasians; the people with darker skin and coarser hair, Negroid; and the people with yellow or brown skin and distinctive folds on their eyelids, Mongoloid. [2]

We know from the movement of humans from all ends of the earth that there had been intermarriage and intermixing for many hundreds of years, therefore, there is only one conclusion to come to and that is humans are all from the same beginnings and the same family. Homo sapiens are what we are; not descendents from animals but made after the image of the Almighty God, Jesus and the Holy Spirit. Most notably in the United States it seems "race" has far reaching implications, and the notion that one group is better than another is still believed by some even in the twenty-first century. Prejudice and discrimination are 'the vicious cycle'; they are mutually reinforcing. Prejudice: is a rigid and irrational generalization concerning a group of people. These attitudes and beliefs have been passed down through families, they can be either positive or negative. Discrimination: is the unequal treatment of certain categories of people. It is also an action word, which also involves behavior (examples: the denial of a job, and housing). Most people have personal preferences that can involve various forms of prejudice. Nevertheless, many Caucasians have some Negroid genes and vice versa for many African Americans.

No matter the reality of mixed groups in America, people are quick to rank and classify each other racially as belonging to one group or the other. There is no scientific research to support assertions that one group is inherently "better" than another. In the 'old' southern states a person with a "drop of Negro blood" was considered to be Black. Today, however, with less caste distinctions in America, the law allows parents to declare the race of their child. This author prays for the day that we will no longer have boxes that ask what race one happens to be, that the only choices will be American or non-American. The division of groups is very divisive. Moore stated that : "Dogs and slaves are named by their masters, Free men name themselves."

Dr. Macionis states: "The 1990 census forms shows that more than 10 million people described themselves by checking more than one racial category." [3]

Hopefully, as time goes on race will become less important in American society and in the world. As so-called mixed marriages are occurring, more and more this author hopes that people will be treated as equals without placing them in racial categories. Dr. Macionis continues:

> Ethnicity is a shared cultural heritage. Members of an ethnic category have common ancestors, language, or religion, that, together, confer a distinctive social identity. [4]

Ethnicity is a far better term than race, simply because it involves more variety, culture, languages and diversity in people's ways of life. This author adheres to the idea that the most criminal of all words in the English language is the word "racism!" Note: Also according to Dr. Macionis the definition of racism is:

> "A powerful and destructive form of prejudice, racism refers to the belief that one racial category is innately superior or inferior to another." [5]

Racism has been widespread in America for centuries. Ideas about the inferiority of race gave credence to slavery and the bondage of humans for hundreds of years; because of this illogical notion. Today, overt racism is far less identifiable than in previous years, mainly due to the egalitarian culture that urges us to evaluate all people, "not by the color of their skin but by the content of their character." However, racism is still "alive and well" in many sections of the United States. Racism is a sickness of the mind that affects the behavioral systems of some people and, to a greater or lesser degree, extends itself throughout all of American society.

It is not unscholarly to say that this racist mindset began in Europe. This is a very dangerous ideology that has been used by man to justify committing inhumane acts upon his fellow man. It is a strong reason why our history was and still is filled with violence.

Sociologists are scientific in their approach to race and ethnicity and tend to present factual information without regard for any one particular belief system as being better or worse than another. Sociology is the science or study of the origin, development, organization, and functioning of human society. Sociology focuses on cultural and environmental factors. It is also the science of the fundamental laws of social relations and institutions.

As an adjunct and Associate Professor this author used Dr. Macionis' textbooks whenever I taught sociology classes. His texts are written very fairly and inclusively for all ethnic (racial) groups, without bias. Dr. Macionis' texts include some of the problems that have plagued various groups in America. I have also personally recommended that anyone teaching sociology use his textbooks rather than any other. We need to know that history is just that, "his-story", and it has usually been written from the European perspective.

Scientists are convinced that the 'term' race is a man made word to further separate the ethnic groups and to assert that one group is superior over another. Again in America we need to really begin to relate to each other as 'humans' without being concerned with the pigment of a person's skin! America—before we can offer solutions to other countries of the world, we need to first fix our own problems within these United States!

Chapter V.

The Re-introduction of Blacks to the Americas (1400-1865)

Originally, Africans sailed over to the Americas and surrounding islands on rafts and small boats. They populated many of the islands and mixed with the Native peoples. All was peaceful; people of different ethnicities coexisting with one another. This went on for hundreds of years prior to Columbus sailing over to "find a land that was already inhabited with people." He did not "discover" anything. A land inhabited by people cannot be discovered. They were never lost to begin with. Columbus was lost. He was headed for India, trying to reach the east by sailing west. He mistakenly called the natives he found in the New World "Indians." Seemingly after a period of religious freedom in the 'New Land' it became necessary to find workers for this vast land. Indentured White slaves were used at first, but they did not work out. Then Native Americans were used but they ran away. Thus, the need for free Africans to be the 'new workers.' Many crew members on the ships had seen the crops and the vegetation growing in Africa, this was the answer to the Europeans dilemma; they forced Africans into slavery. Slavery was not new to Africans as they had their own form of slavery with various tribes. Based on the ancient codes of war, African slavery depended upon the victor in the tribal battles. The losing tribes were enslaved, yet slaves were given every opportunity to coexist with their captors; to work, to live, and to prosper without any stigma attached to their servitude, especially not one based on color. American slavery was the opposite. This was one of the most barbarous and horrific slave practices in modern times. Slaves were in the New World throughout a period of close to 430 years. Africans were maimed, raped, and murdered on a wholesale basis. Over 100 million were taken from Africa to be enslaved, according to *The Original Black Heritage Study Bible;* however, the exact number is unknown. Taking Africans from Africa began as early as the 1400s. Franklin & Moss state:

> When in 1517, Bishop Bartolomo de las Casas advocated the encouragement of immigration to the New World by permitting Spaniards to import African slaves, the trading of men formally began. Las Casas was so determined to relieve Indians of the onerous burden of slavery that he recommended the enslavement of Africans. (Later, he so deeply regretted having taken this position that he vigorously renounced it.) [1]

When reading about slavery in America the books seem to allude to the notion that Africans were all willing to go into slavery, which is far from being true. Many jumped overboard from the ships, others starved themselves to death, others maimed themselves to keep from being useful as slaves. Most importantly there were many slave revolts, but few were written about, including those led by Denmark Vesey, Gabriel Prosser, Nat Turner, and John Brown, the famous White insurrectionist at Harper's Ferry, VA. This author is sure there were many others but the Whites did not want the notoriety because other slaves might revolt.

African familial ties were based on kinship within ethnic groups or tribes. Under American slavery, Blacks weren't grouped along any family lines; they were individually tagged and identified. In other words, the sense of family and community was gone, along with mutual concern for each other. In some respects, this kinship closeness seems to be missing in African American groups to this day. According to Horne:

The large, lightly populated land was the main reason for slavery, based upon the Europeans' greed. No man needs more land than he can farm successfully alone; this policy maintains a natural balance of things. However, the need for more and more land was the primary method for becoming wealthy and powerful, regardless of the upheaval it caused to Native Americans or African slaves. [2]

Greed was the primary reason for the importing of Africans into slavery. Land ownership led to power and thus a great deal of wealth. Horne continues:

This was the European justification for the mass exodus of Africans being re-introduced into the Americas. Because European plantation owners were greedy for land, it was necessary to travel over 8,000 miles to capture and enslave a free people. Black people were also identifiable as slaves and could not blend into the fabric of the European society taking form in America. The battle cry in the new land was for religious freedom and equality but these equalities and freedoms were limited to a select ethnic group. The very rights that Europeans had fled from Europe to seek in the Americas were denied to African slaves. The landowners needed free, slave labor to harvest their crops. Even converting to their own form of Christianity had no bearing on the way slaves were treated by their "masters." [3]

The large plantations provided the opportunity for these "Christians" to import Africans from Africa via thievery. The churches were supporters of human bondage. Even converting to their owner's form of Christianity was no guarantee of better treatment as they were sometimes promised. There were some ministers like John Wesley (a Caucasian) who fought against slavery but they were in the minority along with others that hated slavery, and would later become abolitionists. From *Superman to Man* by J.A. Rogers:

Darwin in his *Descent of Man*, says that when the Negro boys on the east coast of Africa saw Burton, the explorer, they cried out: 'Look at the white man, he looks like a white ape.' The unsophisticated African entertains an aversion to white people,

48

and when accidentally or unexpectedly meeting a white man, he turns and takes to his heels. It is because he feels that he has come upon some unusual or unearthly creature, some hobgoblin or ghost or sprite, and that an aquiline nose, scant lips, and cat-like eyes afflict him. [4]

The Yoruba word for white man is not complimentary. It means 'peeled man.' Stanley, the explorer, said that when he returned from the wilds of Africa he found the complexions of Europeans ghastly 'after so long gazing on rich black and richer bronze' (Stanley was a White man).

Slavery and the theft of millions of Africans shocked and frightened the people of Africa. Many had never seen a "White" person before; it was strange to see the 'pale' skin color. This educator went to Africa and visited two countries, Nigeria and Ghana. Ghana is where two former slave holdings were located. I visited the' slave castles' (which is what they are now called) on Ghana's coast. The two large castles are El Mina, and Cape Coast. The original holding place still exists, and the famous 'door of no return' was also there. A large plaque was placed over the portal stating that once you pass through you would not be able to return. The feeling was grim and dismal even for a tourist to experience. This must have been a very horrific event for the newly captured Africans, to be torn from their lives to face the unknown. There were the eerie sounds of the Atlantic Ocean beating upon the rocks surrounding the castles, truly bone chilling. I could hear crying, wailing, and much sadness in my mind. It was so profound that it felt as if one could reach out and touch the throngs of African people. I attempted to explore the caves and dungeon areas for my classes. However, no matter what I thought I could do, my imagination took me back hundreds of years and I too became one of the captives. Fortunately, the video camera kept running trying to film the exact cave and its interior (my eyes were closed). I was in tears as were other tourists from various countries throughout the world. This was a real firsthand look at the reality of slavery. It was a very emotional and spiritual day for me. Interestingly enough, the upstairs was the living quarters for the captains and the ship crew. There was also a church of sorts where they prayed to God, while human carnage was in the hole hewn out of the rock below that housed men, women and children. To make money the Ghanaian Government had lights installed into the caves and added a few steps, for tourists. The Africans were merely thrown into the hole. There were tiny holes at the top of the caves that provided what air and light they had.

It was an awful example of man's inhumanity towards his fellow man. Racism still haunts America to this day. It has caused insurmountable problems for African Americans. I pray that this sort of brutality is never repeated! The atrocities did not end with the brutalization of the slaves, but it continued—if there were young, pretty women they were held separately and some men used them for sex slaves while they waited for the next ship. If by chance they became pregnant, they were set free, if not they were taken along with the rest of the Africans to become slaves in the New World. Experts have suggested that of the hundred million Africans that were taken, the majority were lost at sea or died from diseases on the long voyages.

The captive Africans came from many areas, and therefore spoke a variety of different languages and dialects; however, they were expected to understand one another, when the only common thread that held them together was the hue of their skin. The common means of communication was the playing of the drums; it was a method of alerting the people when danger was near. The use of drums was stopped shortly after arriving in America. Later, while teaching classes on African slavery, this author had a very different outlook as a result of this very up close and personal experience. I advised all of my students that if the opportunity ever presented itself they too should take a trip to the slave castles. According to Bennett:

> …The European slave trade began in 1444 and continued for more than 400 years. During this period, Africa lost an estimated forty million people. Some twenty million of these men and women came to the New World. Millions more died in Africa during and after their capture or on the ships and plantations…

The slave trade was people living, lying, stealing, murdering and dying. The slave trade was a black man who stepped out of his hut for a breath of fresh air and ended up, ten months later, in Georgia with bruises on his back and a brand on his chest. The slave trade was a black mother suffocating her newborn baby because she didn't want him to grow up a slave. [5]

Africans had to reconnect with their own religion, which was yet another human dignity that had been denied to them; so they met late at night, usually by the riverside, and prayed for freedom and begged God to intercede on their behalf. The slave masters went so far as to take away their languages, dialects and other traditions the slaves needed to remain connected with each other. They were subject to their owners and treated worse than the animals the owner had on his large plantation. The first White indentured slaves ran away and blended into the other Whites of the New World. The second group to be enslaved were Native Americans, but they escaped or resisted, preferring to die of starvation than be enslaved.

Many of the Native Americans ran into the woods, they knew the land and their captors did not. Many Africans did the same; several attempted to jump ship in an attempt to swim back to Africa. Hundreds, perhaps even thousands, died in transit by various means. The slave ships stopped in the islands so that the Masters could break the Africans spirits; by lashing and telling them how to behave. Overseers killed slaves for various infractions even once they had reached America.

It has been estimated that about thirty percent of the Blacks put on ships in Africa died crossing the Atlantic, it being a common practice to throw the sick overboard. Probably half the survivors died soon after reaching America because of the strange food and diseases for which they had no built up immunity. Gerald Horne states:

> Millions of men, women, and children died on the Middle Passage. The cause of this was not, as the texts often imply, suicide, or spoiled food, or homesickness, but epidemics due to foul water, overcrowding, filthy and unsanitary conditions,

not to mention beatings and murders to set an example. The point that the texts neglect in lamenting these "losses" is that this wastage was predictable, and figured quite rationally upon the account books of the merchants who conducted the trade. [6]

It seemed that slaves had no choice in anything that affected their lives. They had no privacy and no control over their lives or their family members' lives. Everything was according to the master and his decisions. John G. Jackson said that over one hundred million Africans were taken from the African continent. The writers of *The Original African Heritage Study Bible* agree. According to Jackson from the 'Introduction to African Civilization':

> All told, the slave trade was responsible for the deaths of over one hundred million Africans. [7]

The White slave masters were not concerned with the loss of slaves on the voyage as their profits would be great enough without attempting to save them all. The slaves were thought to be inexhaustible; therefore, no mercy or pity was shown to slaves no matter what their plight. Slaves were their property "in all that entails" of some Europeans owners. They felt that the Africans, were plentiful and slavery could continue forever.

Some Europeans (generally those of lowest rank and outcasts) were also brought from the Old World as indentured slaves (as prior noted) from the streets and over-crowded prisons. They were prostitutes, thieves, murderers, religious heretics and homeless citizens. These Caucasian slaves easily escaped and blended into the free European society. The indentured slaves at first were both Africans and Whites who worked out their sentences and were often emancipated with a piece of land and a little money to begin their lives anew. However, it did not take long to realize that when White slaves ran it was difficult to find them among the other Whites. But the Africans stood out, and were easily captured. So much for the upstanding Europeans with a Christian perspective for this new country!

Ironically, very little has ever been written concerning European indentured slaves. There were many in the beginning, however, they were not very strong workers and would often run away. This posed a large problem for the masters; they had to find a way to get laborers and insure they would have consistent production. The few Africans that they had along with them were the answer they needed. Crew members from the ships had also seen the farms and workers off the coast of Africa in their travels. African slaves seemed to be the ideal solution to the White man's conundrum.

In 1619, Africans were re-introduced to the New World as indentured servants at first, along with the Europeans. Servitude was also a method of payment for the expense of the trip from Europe and Africa to the Americas. The status of being held as an indentured slave lasted from 1619 until about 1661; then changes were implemented to debase and subject the Black slave to a lifetime of degradation. The Virginia colonists introduced the idea of "lifetime" or perpetual slavery in the late 1600s. Once it became law in Virginia, other southern states followed suit. Slavery was soon converted into perpetual or lifelong rather than having an end date. The state of Virginia was the state that introduced lifelong slavery. Some Africans were never slaves, they came over free and remained that way, others were slaves for a few years and were able to buy their freedom and their families, most of them moved north to Canada, while others moved to northern states where slavery was outlawed. A primary reason for the Civil War was the succession of the northern states from the southern states. Northern states had to pay for labor and the south was getting its labor free. President Lincoln wanted to preserve the union and make the states united: therefore, the Civil War, and the by-product of this event was to free the slaves!

Slavery was an unimaginably barbaric practice—especially by people who took pride in claiming the name of "Christian." Many Christians owned slaves, some were treated well, and others were cruel to their slaves as were the non-Christians. According to Franklin & Moss:

Slave breeding, strangely enough, was one of the most approved methods of increasing agriculture capital. The traditional slave trade was castigated by the slave holding gentry as being inhumane, vicious, and extremely venal; but slave breeding was far more common and much more highly esteemed in the community. One respectable Virginia planter boasted that his women were "uncommonly good breeders" and that he never heard of babies coming as fast as they did on his plantation. Of course, the very gratifying thing about it was that 'every one of them was worth two hundred dollars… the moment they drew breath.' Indeed, breeding was so profitable that many slave girls became mothers at thirteen and fourteen years of age. By the time they were twenty, some young women have given birth to as many as five children. Bounties and prizes were offered for great prolificacy, and in some instances, freedom was granted to mothers who had enriched their masters to the extent of bearing them ten to fifteen children. [8]

Slave breeding was carried on with such indifference to the woman's health or any physical conditions that pregnancy might have caused. All that mattered was that the baby was to be sold. At times women were forced to work in the fields very soon after having given birth. According to Jesse Bernard:

> That women could love children conceived under such circumstances is, in a way quite remarkable, yet many of them were fiercely maternal. "The old overseer, he hate my mammy, 'cause she fight him for beating her children. Why, she git more "whuppings" for that than anything else." Even the children of hated White fathers were cherished. "She was so glad freedom come on before her children come on old enough to sell." Part-White children sold for more than Black children. [9]

A slave mother's love is a hard thing to explain, the children were loved no matter what their origin. But there were also times when a woman would not cut the umbilical cord and the baby would die, the mother would rather the child died than have to grow up a slave and suffer for its entire life. This was not considered to be murder—on the contrary it was seen as an act of love. Slavery was perpetual, and there seemed to be no way of escaping its grasp!

Owners needed a way to be sure of keeping 'slavery' alive, so they sent for Lynch. In 1712, Willie Lynch proposed methods for the plantation owners to control their slaves. He wrote, "I use fear, distrust and envy for control purposes. These methods worked throughout my plantation in the West Indies and it will work throughout the South…

"I assure you that distrust is stronger than trust, and envy is stronger than adulation, respect or admiration." [From a copy of The Willie Lynch Document written in 1712]

On the top of Lynch's list came age, followed by: "color" or shade, intelligence, stature, sex, the size of the plantation, status and attitude of the master, whether the slaves lived in a valley, hill, the direction of their residence; whether they had fine or coarse hair or were tall or short. [10]

Imagine how difficult it is for an intelligent person to hear Blacks calling each other names, most of those derogatory words were used at lynching's such as the word n…..! No doubt the word for lynching came from Willie Lynches' name. This is a very sad state of affairs, and Blacks need to understand how detrimental it is to use such deadly words towards each other. Lynch continues:

> The Black slave, after receiving this indoctrination shall carry on and will become self-debasing and will perpetuate these negatives for hundreds of years, maybe even thousands. [10]

After 148 years the negativity, distrust and envy continues, to some degree, even today. This is a very sad but truthful commentary on some African Americans or Blacks. Lynch went on to say, "Slave owners must pit the young against the old slaves, and use skin tone against them. Color has always proven to be problematic for the slaves."

Unfortunately, this is still true today, for some African Americans cannot stand to see those of their group with fair skin and softer hair. The adages from Lynch still permeate some African American communities; although it has lessened now that Miss America can be an African American of a darker hue; and not look almost white. With this kind of indoctrination it is no wonder there are multiple problems within the African American community even to this very day. In modern times these feelings of so-called "being close to White" are not in vogue, and all shades of African Americans are now treated the same. It was refreshing however, to see a very dark-skinned Miss America, after beautiful Vanessa Williams who looked almost White with her green eyes, and soft hair. Vanessa Williams, you are truly beautiful, but my point still needed to be made. According to Van Sertima:

> In the beginning, only male Africans were brought to the Americas. Later, it was decided that African women should be imported so that Black males could mate with their "own kind." Early on in slavery White women lived with or married Black slaves. This did not seem to be problematic in the beginning. However, the White masters did not cease from sleeping with slave women and having children with them. In contrast, interracial marriages, particularly between some European men and African women, were common, sanctioned and encouraged in Latin America, even under slavery. [11]

There is no such thing as a "race." The term is merely a man-made form of delineation without any real validity. White males had the ability to do whatever they desired to the Black slave woman because they were the law. The Black woman and her husband (or man) had no recourse; they were powerless to protect themselves or their children. While some White masters would sell their bi-racial offspring, others would keep and free their children upon their deaths; and often leave them land, houses and money. This act was called "manumission." That is how many Blacks (after slavery) were able to have a positive start toward becoming self-sufficient. There were always free Black men in America during slavery; they managed to escape to Canada or to other northern states that did not uphold slavery.

William (Bill) Grimke-Drayton is my friend. He lives in Christchurch, Dorset, in the United Kingdom. I came across his article on the Internet and he gave me permission to add portions of his article into my book. Born and raised in England, Mr. Drayton has written an article on his ancestors' connection to the slave trade in Charleston, South Carolina. Drayton has taken several trips to his family's plantation where he has met with distant Black relatives for the first time. From Mr. Drayton's article about his American genealogy:

> The Drayton's first settled in the Carolina colony in 1679. They became one of the wealthiest plantation-owning families, with 30 properties. The Grimke's arrived in the early 18th century. My great-great-great-great aunts, Sarah and Angelina Grimke, campaigned against slavery and for women's rights. After the death of his first wife, their brother Henry Grimke took Nancy Weston, one of his slaves, as his wife in an illegal, mixed marriage. Together, they had three sons; Archibald, Francis and John. Archibald was involved in law and politics, whereas Francis became a Presbyterian minister in Washington, D.C. They fought for equal rights for all. It seemed that all the children grew up to be successful in life. [12]

This is but one example from slavery, however, most Black women were still obligated to serve their White masters as though they never had any children by them. Often, the master would impregnate his wife and a Black female at about the same time so the slave could wet-nurse for the White woman. It was considered unsightly for proper White women to suckle their children and many were too weak after childbirth to care for their infants. Instead of nursing and coddling her own babies, the slave had to provide the White child with nurture. The slave woman was trusted with a new life, but could not be a mother to her own babies because she had to work for the master's family. What an upside-down state of affairs! Blacks were not good enough to be considered human, yet they were good enough to nurse and care for the master's children. The Black slave women breast-fed the babies of their owners. Also, they were expected to give medications to the children and they prepared the food; however they could not read or write. What's wrong with this scenario? Interestingly enough, Rogers, in his book, *Superman to Man,* states:

> ...when the two races meet in Europe each of the people in question can learn something ennobling from the other, and ennobling influences have no color. When a Caucasian reads Terence, Aesop, Dumas, Pushkin, George Douglas John and Jesse Fauset; admires the paintings of Tanner, Scott or Harper; or listens to the music of Coleridge-Taylor, Rosamond Johnson, Dett or Burleigh, he has associated with what for a better name we will call Negro Thought. If one has association with author's works then why not give credit to the authors themselves? [13]

Historically, this information is barely known because most people have been taught that these were Europeans of distinguished nobility. In this author's opinion if some of these persons had common names like Smith or Williams' one would wonder if their climb to fame would have happened so undaunted. Most books declare Pushkin to be Russian, Dumas a darker skinned European; much like a Clark Gable and Aesop to be a Greek mentor. They could and would be described as anything but what they were: people of African descent. There was a time in ancient history when marriage was between two people and it was not discouraged no matter their ethnicities. However, in America laws forbade marriage between members of different 'racial'/ethnic groups. Amazingly if the contributors are called by a different group than the one that they represent, that makes it fine. The world gets the benefit and no one is the wiser! Laws were written in the judicial books that strictly prohibited marriage between Whites and Blacks during the earlier years of slavery. It was not until June 12, 1967 that the last laws against interracial marriages were struck down by the U.S. Supreme Court in Loving vs. Commonwealth of Virginia. The relationships between Whites and Blacks that culminate in marriage are still viewed as deviant by many people in America even today. According to Dr. Billingsley:

> An ex-slave has told of getting married on one plantation: when you married, you have to jump over a broom three times. Dat was de license. If master seen two slaves together too much he

would tell-em dye was married. Hit didn't make no difference if you wanted to or not, he would put you in de same cabin and make you live together, Marsa used to sometimes pick our wives fo' us. If he didn't have on his place enough women for the men, he would wait on de side of de road till a big wagon loaded with slaves come by. Den Marsa would stop de old nigger-trader and buy you a woman. Wasn't no use tryin' to pick one, cause Marsa wasn't gonna pay but so much for her. All he wanted was a young healthy one who looked like she could have children, whether she was purty or ugly as sin. [14]

Marriages for Blacks happened when the masters said so. If slaves spent any time together the master would say they were married and they would carry out the practice of 'jumping the broom' three times. But this in itself would not keep the master from selling them apart. Franklin & Moss write:

Few owners were sufficiently insensitive to human decency to admit that they were willing to divide slave families by sale. As a matter of fact, families were frequently advertised as being for sale together, but they were not always sold together. Slaves often brought higher prices when sold separately. The large numbers of single slaves on the market bears testimony to the rather ruthless separation of families that went on during the slave period. [15]

Under slavery, some White men even sold their own bi-racial offspring in this trade of humans in order to gain economic wealth. Slavery was basically an economic system. "Slave marriages" were of no consequence because at any time the master wanted a wife of a slave, he just took her and laid with her. The women were utterly defenseless. The male slave could not protect his woman or his bed. This is a prime example of how dehumanizing the state of slavery really was.

When slavery finally ended, marriage licenses were in very high demand among Blacks. They wanted legal, officially licensed marriages; not the 'jumping the broom' practice that the planters told them to do. In Africa, jumping the broom was a genuine part of the matrimonial ritual, but in America it was seen as a put-down compared to the "real marriage ceremony" with papers and licenses. Some modern Blacks will still 'jump the broom' after the usual ceremony as a symbolic gesture to the past, giving respect and honor to an African tradition. They usually hang the decorative broom on the family room wall to show it to all who visit the home.

Finally, with the invention of the cotton gin, one would have thought this machine would drastically reduce the need for large numbers of slaves. However, just the opposite occurred when larger production plantations developed. This phenomenon made the need for slaves even greater. Slavery grew into a more lucrative business than ever before. There was no need to treat slaves as humans, in fact, they became known as "beasts of burden." If a slave died, another was easily purchased, thus, slaves were seen as an inexhaustible resource. The myth soon spread among the Whites that Blacks had no "souls" and were, therefore, not human so it did not matter how cruelly they were treated. This carried over into religion, which meant that, even if a slave became a Christian by the European definition, they would still remain a slave. With the notion that Blacks had no "souls," it meant Blacks did not have human qualities that Whites were bound to respect. There was no limit to how long slaves could work in the fields. On the large plantations, masters continued working their slaves until they died or were killed for some infraction.

Some Whites took absolutely no responsibility for their behavior and they seemingly had no conscience about their treatment of Blacks at all. The taking of Africans was a "big economic business," as the economic wealth for the planters was built upon the backs of the slaves. Like their livestock, slaves were considered property, better known as chattel. While a few Black men taught their children to fight back, even if it meant their deaths, the majority resigned themselves to just accept their fate. It seems, however, there were always people who would not accept conditions as they were, and tried to defend themselves. Europeans neglected to write about the many Africans who would rather die than become slaves. Many slave uprisings were not written about for fear this type of rebellion would entice other slaves to rebel. Before slavery was over, slaves would often run away to try to find their loved ones.

After slavery, it was a celebration to find their relatives who had been sold off; and to marry legally and put their families back together. Recent arguments denying slave breeding by some students of history cannot successfully refute these and other contemporary testimonies regarding the practice of slave breeding. Since the domestic slave trade and breeding were essentially economic (not humanitarian) activities it is not surprising to find that, in the sale of slaves, there existed the persistent practice of dividing families. Husbands were separated from their wives and mothers were separated from their children. This is not to say there was never any respect for basic human rights or ample sentimentality to prevent the separation of families; it would have been good business to keep families together. Sadly, since people sold and bought slaves largely for economic reasons, most of the time they eschewed the civilities that would have frowned upon family separation. These laws, if enforced, would have done much to ameliorate the conditions of slavery, but were almost wholly disregarded. In many slave states, they didn't even have any such provisions. Children were sold as soon as they were weaned, others when they could walk, and still others when it was determined they could work (between 7-10 years old). This was a horrendous way to have to live; slavery was extremely harsh for millions of Black people. America owes a great debt to their darker brothers and sisters in America for the many years of free labor and the blood, sweat and tears it took to build this country into what it is today. Not many books give any credit to Blacks but they should. The apologies are fine, but reparations would have been better. The Japanese in World War II were given some monetary benefits, but never the builders of this mighty nation of freedom and liberty!

Finally, in January 1863, President Lincoln handed down the Emancipation Proclamation, which was implemented in only a few states at first, and finally enforced in 1865 for the remaining slave holding states. Blacks in America were finally "Free at Last!" This should have meant the beginning of a new life for former Black slaves, but there were still some Whites with negative attitudes that would stifle and hinder Blacks in their attempts to achieve and prosper. Most of this was systemic discrimination keeping Blacks from employment, housing and other means of survival. Many of these unresolved problems for Black people still remain as many encounter negative behaviors on a daily basis. The practice of "Jim Crow" in the northern cities, along with discriminatory practices throughout the nation kept Black people in a lower socioeconomic level. Blacks have been free for 146 years (148 if one were to count from 1863 rather than from 1865). However the vestiges of racism continue to haunt Blacks in America even into the 21st century!

Nothing shall be impossible unto you
(Matthew 17:20)

Chapter VI.

While Moving Forward: The Black Family After Slavery (1865-Present)

Ironically, the Emancipation Proclamation was a wonderful legal document that freed Blacks, but it neglected to provide them protection. Further, it seems this gesture was not necessarily for the benefit of Blacks. According to Dr. Billingsley:

> White institutions have been instituted for the advancement of Whites even when they have espoused causes that seemingly focus on the welfare of Blacks." For example: President Lincoln wanted to "save the union;" even though the slaves could probably gain their freedom as a result of the Civil War. [1]

Franklin and Moss stated:

> In his startling conclusions regarding the crucial questions of freed slaves Alexis de Tocqueville stated nearly 150 years ago, "It was not for the good of the Negroes, but for that of the Whites, that measures are taken to abolish slavery in the United States." [2]

As de Tocqueville stated, the abolishment of slavery was not in the interest of human rights, but profit. It seems most things the White man does are in the interest of his wealth. It was a known fact that the division between the White Northerner and the White Southerner was based on money; slavery itself was an economic venture. Whatever the real reason, slavery was finally ended, and Blacks were truly grateful. Of course, freedom had advantages for the Black family; marriages among Blacks were legalized and recorded. While family members were still whipped, run out of town or murdered, they could no longer be sold away from their loved ones. The period following emancipation was hard for the ex-slaves. They were homeless and did not know where their loved ones were; many starved to death during their search. According to Franklin and Moss:

> Emancipation was, for some Negro slaves, a major life altering predicament for them… Reconstruction was a disastrous failure. However, there were 'windows of opportunity' that enabled a large number of families to survive; some managed to achieve stable forms of family life… A few Negroes were able to achieve a high degree of social prominence…" [3]

However, many Blacks were without food, housing, or employment when they were freed. One of the first things that slaves did was to look for their loved ones who had been sold throughout the state to other plantations and/or out of the state. Most freed men wanted to legally get married with a ring, and a license. It was a very hard period for the freed Blacks, but they were determined to survive.

The Freedmen's Bureau was established in 1865 for the newly freed slaves—offering them food, education, shelter, clothing, medicine and skills for "doing for themselves." It also built hospitals and schools. Sadly, the bureau did not last long enough to really help Black people and poor Whites become independent. It ended in 1872. There was no more Master to answer questions or to tell the Blacks what to do. General Sherman had written a Proclamation giving 40 acres and a mule to all freed Black families, land was set aside in Georgia and Florida for these settlements. However, after a few years the Proclamation was rescinded and the land was given back to White farmers. Blacks were once again left without anything.

Note: There is (at the time of writing) a program being run by Bishop Henry Williams in Oakland, California called "Restitution/ Reparation." Williams has a large following nationwide and they have been to Washington, D.C. to talk with various lawmakers. To date nothing has been resolved. President Obama had once stated that he is not in favor of reparations. Perhaps, some African American leaders can convince him that it would be a benefit as our ancestors built this wonderful country with free slave labor. Hopefully the Restitution / Reparations Program will be successful.

The Reconstruction period was a government program set up to restore the States that had succeeded from the union, Rebuilding the South houses and land, restore owners to their legal land. This period lasted for twelve years. Again it was up to the slave states to work with the freed slaves. After the Reconstruction period ended, another form of servitude was put in place called sharecropping. This was just another disguise for the continuation of slavery endured for hundreds of years. Some ex-slaves were kept on at the old plantations and some were held there against their will. Again, they were told what to do and had to work for the former owners or be put in jail, or severely beaten. When the sharecroppers finished harvest and seeds for next year's crops, they had to wait until the plantation owners tallied up the proceeds. Usually, they were told there was no money for them, but they could have some of the harvest and seed for the next year's crops. No matter how much money the Black families made for the Whites, they ended up with nothing!

This sharecropping system continued until International Harvester made a cotton-picking machine, perfected in 1944, which replaced hundreds of Blacks. Now, Blacks did not have any work to do so many left for the north.

The "Great Migration" in America occurred between 1915 and 1940. Seemingly unbeknownst to the Whites, five million Blacks left the rural south for the "Promised Land" of the north. When Blacks reached the northern cities, they were met with another limitation called "Jim

Crow," the term given to discriminatory, racist attitudes of Whites in the north. Blacks were relegated to live in the worst parts of the cities and to work for low-paying, menial jobs. To thousands of Blacks living in the north, this was freedom, and they would not trade it for the southern lifestyles they had left behind. The ugly head of racism, was still doing damage to deter and stop the progress of the Black family. At the same time, Blacks were given rights by the Supreme Court and the 'laws of the land' were refusing to cooperate. In other words, there were de jure laws on the legal books, and there were de facto laws that was the 'real' law which Blacks faced daily. That included keeping them from jobs, housing and little or no educational opportunities.

It seems that Blacks were not important in America, however, three out of the twelve Landmark Decisions of the Supreme Court involved them. And the fourth involved a young Mexican man by the name of Miranda. This author will offer a brief synopsis of these cases. The Landmark years were: 1857, 1896, 1954, and 1966.

In 1857 there was a Supreme Court decision called the Dred Scott versus Stanford case. This decision involved a man named Dred Scott who had been a slave in the south. When his master took him to the north, into a free state he wanted his freedom. But, the master refused to grant him his freedom. This case finally made it all the way to the Supreme Court where the Justices decided that there was nothing a Black could say or do that the White man was obliged to honor or respect. In other words the treatment in slavery was whatever the White man said it should be.

In other words America was founded on the Bible and its Holy scriptures, however, through the years America evolved into a slave holding nation after the White man had too much land to cultivate himself. It seemed that the Europeans were fleeing Europe to have religious freedoms, only to enslave a free people from Africa solely because of their color and the need for laborers to build this nation. The laws in America soon declared that all Africans were to be legally held in bondage perpetually. President Abraham Lincoln wrote the Emancipation Proclamation in 1862 and it became law to free the slaves. On January 1, 1863, all the slave states near Washington, D.C., were set free. But, it was as late as June 1865, when slaves were freed in distant states like Texas. Therefore, we have the celebration of Juneteenth once per year on June 19, celebrating freedom from slavery. There is much fun and singing, games, African American art, handmade items, tee-shirts and soul food to share. Most cities throughout America have them and it is a positive event to attend for all ethnic groups. Now on a very somber note from Franklin & Moss:

> From 1889 to 1922, twenty-five riots took place where 3,436 Black people were lynched or murdered. James Weldon Johnson called the summer of 1919 the "Red Summer," due to the high number of Blacks being killed. Many Black men, who had just returned from World War I and only wanted jobs, were lynched; still wearing the military uniforms they wore while defending their country. American diplomats did nothing to aid or protect them once they returned from the war. [4]

This is a sad commentary on how Blacks were treated at this period in American history. Many others have been lynched prior to and after this period of time. Some Whites just could not stand to see a Black man with a weapon. The Black men had just returned home from fighting in the war for America. What a horrible homecoming! Defending freedom for this country and yet being denied freedom for themselves. Blacks were being lynched by the thousands, and nothing was done about it! Blacks have served in every war that America has been involved in. From the time of the Boston Massacre (Revolutionary period) a Black was one of the first to be killed. And every War since, Blacks have joined in great numbers. Yet their service seemingly went unnoticed. Many hundreds and perhaps even thousands have died in the various wars for America.

What is one of the most horrendous legacies of slavery? Lynchings of course. The murder of Emmitt Till (1954), is an example of a lynching. A more recent lynching was James Byrd (1998), in Jasper, Texas. Are lynching's still going on? It depends on whether or not it gets publicized. Many horrific things have happened to Blacks and yet were never brought to the media. This author believes the problem continues under any guise—some Whites will use any excuse to do harm to Blacks.

In 1896, the Supreme Court passed Plessy versus Ferguson. This law became known as the "Separate but Equal" clause which meant segregation was legal all over the United States. The pattern that was firmly established under slavery continued as "just the way that things were done." The entire nation knew the races were separate but never equal. This decision was based on Homer Plessy who was light skinned and had nice hair. He looked White, however, the train driver knew his family and knew that he was a member of the Black group. When asked to sit at the back of the train car, Mr. Plessy replied, "I am as white as you are!" The Supreme Court decision decided that segregation was the right way for the "races" to coexist. This made it very difficult for Blacks to get ahead and to obtain a proper education. The Black family was determined to survive, so all of the family members worked, including Black women who worked in White women's kitchens and cared for their children. Black men, for the most part, worked at low-paying jobs that the White men no longer wanted to perform. With both parents working, the grandmother took over the care of the children. Yet even with both parents working, they were barely able to feed their families. Segregation was still the law in the south and some of the north. While this presented numerous problems for the Black family, it did not deter their determination to survive. Emerging scholars of color could no longer ignore the Black family, as White scholars had previously done. With support from White institutions, these few Black scholars, and a handful of Whites, wrote about Black family life. Many of these new-breed sociologists were concerned about the real problems facing the Black family. They concluded, after careful research, that racism was the major contributing factor affecting the Black family.

Their contributions were factual and accurately written. The main writers of Black literature were historians and sociologists, many of whom came from Chicago Universities. E. Franklin Frazier, a noted sociologist at the University of Chicago, wrote several books on the Black family. As Jesse Bernard and others often concluded, information was most significant when written by an individual of the group being written about—this author agrees.

In the early 20th century Black households were intact with nuclear families; a father, mother and children. The majority of babies were born into households with both parents. It is very important to note that the family was (and is) one of the most important Black institutions aside from the church. Despite the numerous problems the Black family faced, it was determined to survive, despite hundreds of men and women going into segregated units of the military. Franklin and Moss write:

> Jobs, housing and education were always problems for Negroes. When Negro men returned for the military from World War I… they were very disappointed to have gone to war to protect their country, and upon their arrival home, many were beaten and their guns taken away from them… Also many could not find jobs even though they were trained for good jobs, the jobs were denied them, basically because of racism which tends to overtly and directly affect one's life and livelihood. Most Blacks had little to no formal education other than what they might have received from the Military. These were very hard, and discouraging times in Black men's lives. No matter how hard the low paying jobs, dirty and sometimes dangerous, the men worked to take care of their families. [5]

In 1954, Brown versus The Board of Education was taken to the Supreme Court. This case involved a girl named Linda Brown; who was denied admittance to her local school because of her skin color. She had to be bussed across town to a Black school. Her parents took the case to the Supreme Court. The decision was that segregated schools were inherently evil; hence all public schools were to be integrated. This did not include private schools. Now, according to the law, there would be no more 'separate but equal schools' (when in fact they never stopped). This was followed shortly after by the 1964 Civil Rights Laws which opened housing, eating in public restaurants and the ability to sit on various forms of transportation, without having to always sit in the very back. Interestingly enough most young Blacks opt to sit at the very back when it is no longer mandatory. This author has never really understood this fact!

The fourth landmark decision involved a Mexican American. Mr. Ernesto Miranda versus Arizona. The Supreme Court decision was in 1966, when Miranda was accused of raping a mildly retarded young White woman. He was not given any rights at all: the right to remain silent, having a lawyer present, knowing that anything that you say or do can be held against you in a court of law. He did not speak English and he was not provided with an interpreter. The mistreatment that happened to Mr. Miranda happened on a regular basis to Black and Latino youth, but thanks to him, the laws; even though stringent when it came to dealing with minorities, at last had to acknowledge their rights.

Presently, there are many Blacks in prison after being denied their rights, and nothing has been done about it. There are agencies today that are trying to free these men who have been falsely imprisoned.

Note: The Black families were stable until the number of new births among Blacks began to decline in the 1960s. After this period, many Black couples opted not to have children or only one or two. This was due to the economics involved with caring for a large family in uncertain financial times. However these families were intact with a mother and a father.

The decline began about forty years ago and continues today; even considering the high numbers of unwed teenage mothers within the Black population. One factor contributing to this decline is the unavailability of marriage-aged Black males due to incarceration, homosexuality and interracial marriages. Other factors include high infant mortality, increased number of abortions, and the increased use of contraceptives. Unfortunately, single motherhood has also become an accepted phenomena. This is seen as a negative in America, as most other groups still adhere to a nuclear family. With the proper examples and instruction this too can be turned around for the betterment of the Black group.

Many books were published around 40 years ago to do with Blacks. Some were 'a self-fulfilling prophecy', as most of American society believed what they read and saw in the media. Sadly, some Blacks also believed the 'hype'; that is the pattern of a "beaten" people who, through the many years of maltreatment, have internalized negatives about themselves and their self-worth. After hundreds of years, it is very difficult to change these self-perceptions in a just a few generations. Yet, change has begun to "blossom" throughout the Black society in America. Black parents always wanted their children to have a better life than they had. Previously, most of the Black youth were properly dressed and lived in well-maintained homes or apartments; cleanliness was demanded. These children were taught morality, manners, and to take pride in their appearance. Somehow, some of these fundamentals seem to have been lost in recent years. The damage to the Black group has come not only from physical abuse but also from mental abuse. For example, in slavery, the Black man was emasculated, not only physically but also psychologically, to "protect the White world." This psychological damage was most severe when it was internalized and passed on to future generations. Black slave men were used to sire children for trade, creating a disconnection with the role of parenting. Regrettably, this trend seemingly has also carried over into the present times. Once freed, the institution perpetuated this emasculation by denying Black men decent jobs, housing, and other means of supporting their families.

In contrast, an important role among Blacks during slavery (that has all but vanished) was the role of the granny, "the guardian of the generations" (Frazier, 1963). The position of the oldest woman in a family was, traditionally, an extremely important one as the matriarch. The grandmother played an important part even under slavery, and was "highly esteemed by both the slaves and the masters." She was wisdom personified and the keeper of the family history, to be passed on to future generations. In the master's house, she was very often called "mammy" or "granny" whose history and tradition have been idealized because of her loyalty and affection. Because of her intimate relations with the Whites, "all the family secrets," Calhoun observes, were in her keeping as the defender of the family honor. The ties of affection between her and her charges were never outgrown. Often, she was the confidential advisor to older members of the household; to young mothers, she was an authority on first babies; both Black and White.

The Black 'granny' was a true matriarch; a profoundly powerful and stabilizing female head of family. Even today, film and media often contain the images of strong black women in roles of "big mama" or the 'granny'. In modern times the most successful youth are reared in a home with a grandmother living with them or one that lives nearby. Most parents have to work to survive and the grandmother is the one with her wisdom rearing the children. My heart-felt thanks go to my grandmother and to all the grandmothers of the world who help to instill a sense of purpose and self-worth in children to help them to make better choices in life. However, in some homes the Black woman has had to be the mother and the father for her children. More recent-ly, the Black woman has had to assume some roles originally assigned for males, especially when it comes to employment.

Primarily, it is still racism that hinders Black men, in a planned ef-fort to keep them in subservient roles. Therefore, many of the family duties have fallen upon the woman to fulfill. This trend has, unfortu-nately, been pervasive and problematic for the Black family. Having said that, there are some Black men who refuse to get an education and also refuse to work; they are "professional baby-makers." They hop from bed to bed making babies but not caring for any of them. This has got to stop as there are far too many children growing up without positive father figures in their lives. Parents need to teach their boys it is wrong to impregnate a girl and then leave her caring for the baby. Parents further need to teach their young girls that "saving themselves" for marriage is a wonderful thing to do. Boys do not 'love you,' they just 'lust after you.' And that is the real four letter word for: "I 'love' you baby." Some churches have abdicated their burden to teach and train the young. Churches should have more groups/programs geared towards young people to help them to live in this environment today according to Biblical teachings. Without our youth our churches tend to die.

Providing for the family is a role left to the Black women inherited from slavery because, at any time, the master could decide to sell the man off to another plantation. And often the master "would sire" the Black males out to insure his slave population would continue to grow and the man had no responsibility for their children. Would it be possible for someone to inform young Black men that slavery is over! If the family was to survive, it had to depend upon the woman, who had to be strong and stable. These traits have somehow been seen as negative, rather than positive, traits. Usually, there was always a granny around to share her wisdom with the mother and the children

Black women were the stable force in the Black family down through the generations. The Black woman has had to be strong and willing to keep the family together in spite of the formidable circumstances in which she found herself. There was a conspiracy of sorts against the Black man. He was always being called "boy" and then, when he was old and his hair had turned gray, he was called "uncle." These insulting names only tended to diminish the Black males' status in his family and in the work force. With ineffective weapons, the Black male had to wage a constant battle against an arsenal of barriers. Education and training are much-needed devices in this conflict, yet they alone do not make the man. The Black man must draw on his personal strength and fortitude to sustain himself and his family against the odds.

Researchers have speculated that the female oriented household has contributed to the emasculation of the Black male. However, there is usually a grandfather, a boyfriend, a male teacher or a scout leader who demonstrates the characteristics of male role models. Some Black men have adopted a so-called "Black" way of walking, talking, dressing, and even acting, to support the position that they are men; in every aspect of the word.

There has always tended to be the Black male who was belligerent, rude, arrogant, and hostile in his dealings with women, either Black or White. These 'bad Blacks' were usually known in various neighborhoods and most people avoided them. Then, there is the professional Black male that is highly educated and has successfully navigated the waters leading to wealth, position and some status. Attempting to reach out and help others will not damage the struggle made to 'arrive.' Sometimes a professional Black male will help a member or two of his family to obtain success. Usually, even with some of the trappings of success there is always the threat that one could lose everything if one attempted to make waves or become known as a 'trouble maker.' In other words the need to share the wealth has not been a reality in most Black areas. Of the many famous athletes, singers and actors/actresses, some have made great strides to reach out to other less fortunate Blacks. Among the known contributors are Oprah Winfrey and Dr. William (Bill) Cosby. Other famous Blacks have simply claimed the fame and moved on with their own lives without regard for anyone else; and most married White women. The fact is that none of the privileges that are taken for granted would have been possible without the sacrifices of Blacks marching, protesting, and struggling for some semblance of equality. As my mother Ella would always say 'down through the years.' The Black group had many "bridge builders" to be eternally grateful to, among those were Dr. Banneker, Dr. Carver, Justice Marshall, and Dr. King.

Dr. Martin Luther King, Jr. was truly a great hero a wonderful American with his undying struggle to help the masses and the down trodden. He also worked to obtain equality and justice for Blacks and other groups. He was also concerned with *all poor people*. Thanks to his efforts along with others' there are more opportunities available today than ever before for most Americans. The struggle continues because the root systemic problems have not been thoroughly eradicated from America.

In the 1960s, a new kind of student emerged in American society who wanted to know more. He/she raised questions concerning Blacks and the inadequately explained answers that Whites had been providing up until now. This was a time when Blacks were "Black and proud," and wanted to find their "roots." Alex Haley and his book Roots did much to contribute to the flood of new materials on the market on Blacks from a Black perspective. Just a few years before this time, it would have been "fighting words "if a Black person was called "Black." It seemed that when James Brown sung out "I'm Black and I'm proud!" There was a new change that arrived in the Black communities throughout America; now most Blacks were proud of their heritage, and their looks. Some merchants in White America were not happy, they were losing money on hair straightening products, clothes and shoes, pursuing the "Barbie" look. Up until now Black women had dressed similar to Whites, and had their hair styled to be straight. Some Whites found this new phenomenon to be very disturbing. Blacks were wearing their hair natural with "Afros" and African type clothing. Everything was done to regain their African History that was once seen as "negative;" it was now being thought of as positive. Some writers and news persons were asking questions of Blacks attempting to find out what was going on. This was amazing and unsettling to many in White America. One of the questions that was asked was, "What do you people want?" Now African Americans were opening their own stores and providing the African clothes many times cheaper directly from African merchants.

Some writers focused upon poverty. The more they investigated the more they found that Blacks were over-represented as being poor. Especially since their numbers made up a smaller percentage of the population in America. This is also true of the prison scenario. Black males make up over 60 percent of all the persons imprisoned, and yet we are told Blacks make up only about 13 percent of the total population here in America. One can quickly assume that something is not quite right with our judicial system. These poverty experts soon found that there was a connection between poverty and the Black family. If the statistics were correct then the majority of people on the welfare rolls had to be White, as they were reported to have been the majority in America. When this fact was finally fathomed out; less was said about people being on welfare. Welfare was only news when Blacks were suspected as being the largest users of the system.

The Black family was always important to Blacks in America. The extended family was an important aspect of the Black family, which included the grandparents, cousins, aunts, or uncles. In other words, there was always someone there to help with the children and teach them their morals and values. The extended family concept came from Africa. The notion that other family members would live in one house and share the rearing of the children, keeping traditions and values instilled in the youth. Note: this quote was not originally from from Mrs. Hillary Clinton: "It takes village to raise a child." This is a very old African proverb meaning that all the community shared in the rearing of children. This practice, however, was foreign to Whites in America. Of course, it was viewed as deviant behavior. Any behavior or pattern not from Europe was seen as outside "the norm." Therefore, it should be studied and researched. The Black family stayed under the micro-scope seemingly for many years.

In 1965, Daniel P. Moynihan wrote a devastating book, *The Pathology of the Negro Family*. The basic premise was that the Black family was pathological in a nature endemic to Blacks. Meaning it was diseased when compared to the Caucasian group. The media disected the Black family constantly, the focus being directed upon the on the female head of household and babies being born without fathers in the home. The 1960s census single parent chart was high for Black females as well as for White females. There was no mention however of the 75% intact (both parents in the home) Black families in America. This report, unfortunately, became a "self-fulfilling prophecy." Moynihan and other sociologists at the time saw the Black family as being deviant from the White family structure.

This report further stated the high poverty levels among Black single females. However, all Black people faced poverty, prejudice, and historical subjugation because of their skin color. Sociologists called the poor women's plight 'the feminization of poverty'. This held doubly true for the Black mothers in America. Many studies have been done concerning this sociological phenomenon in a country where racism is "as American as apple pie." When Whites are at poverty levels, they only face the disadvantage of poverty; not both poverty and racism. Black women have traditionally been the "mainstay," if you will, for the Black family; the major reason being that racism has been largely perpetrated against the Black male.

In 1964 and '65, when the Civil Rights laws were passed, the 'Separate but Equal' doctrine was finally dismantled. Blacks could ride in the front of the bus, rather than the back; and Blacks could eat in restaurants without having to eat outside in the back; and Blacks can now sleep in hotels and motels. However, many aspects of segregation still persist in various, mainly covert ways as opposed to blatant ones. There are still vestiges of segregation that keep Blacks from obtaining a proper education; especially men.

There is a wide disparity between the education of Black youth and White youth in this country. There are vast differences in test scores; in many schools in America. Why? The bottom line is still associated with various forms of racism. The more blatant forms of brutality came in the form of "open season for killing Black males." In recent years young Blacks were being killed by drugs, drive by killings, shootings by themselves and/or the police!

Examples would be the Rodney King beating and the police killings of numerous young Black men throughout the nation. In fact, Black youth were targeted to the extent that Black authors began writing about the possible extinction of Black males in America. For many months newspaper headlines were about how the police were shooting Black youth (always in self-defense according to the officer that did the shooting). The police were/are acquitted even when the victim was shot in the back(!); or shot without carrying a weapon, even though the police said that the victim threatened them with what they thought was a weapon. Sometimes it seems that a Black male is a threat to the police merely by being Black. Some Black men became increasingly discouraged with the continuous discrimination and oppression that plagued their existence on every level. The Black family as a unit began to crumble. The Black woman was left with the responsibility of financially, mentally, and physically supporting the family. This time period witnessed a rise in criminal behavior, which led to the incarceration of numerous Black men. This further compounded the problems that the Black family was and is still experiencing.

The years of racial discrimination, oppression, and degradation caused many Black people to lose faith in God, the church, and themselves. Too many Black families today are headed by single women and by children who are bearing children at a time when they are incapable of caring for themselves. At the same time, Black boys have become discouraged and have resorted to the so-called "gangster lifestyle" of drugs, sex and violence. The "rap" music tends to put down women in a very negative manner! There were and still are periods of "drive-by shootings," in many areas in the minority sections of America. Black-on-Black crime was/is in the headlines on a regular basis. This devastating situation of Black-on-Black crime has almost claimed an entire generation of Black children. Alcohol and other hard drugs permeate the Black community, seemingly with the blessing of the legal system. Nothing much is done when illegal drugs are in the minority neighborhoods, yet, another stance is taken when these illegal drugs include "White children." Where do these drugs come from? Are Blacks flying planes from one country to another to pick up the drugs? (This author does not think so). These drugs are a large part of our American economy (the underground society). If the American government wanted to halt drugs, it would be stopped today. Illegal drugs have been placed in these United States to eradicate young Black men and other minorities, or so it seems. The illegal drugs are brought into America on planes, ships and sometimes boats. Most drugs are brought by wealthy persons with the ability to rent or own the mechanisms to bring in the contraband. However, it ends up on the streets of the ghettos and the barrios throughout the nation. These poor hustlers are being jailed and sent to prison by the hundreds; they are the "small fish." Very seldom do the persons at the top get caught, which is very unfair and the punishment works against the "penny anti" street thugs. The real perpetrators are still in the illegal drug business. And the "top men"(drug pushers) are very wealthy, usually White, and living in upper class neighborhoods throughout America.

Since the 1980s, and up to the present day, there have been many interracial marriages. These marriages have produced "so-called" biracial offspring; they make up a large segment of the total American population. This adds to the total number of Blacks not including the many thousands of "mulattos" who were born throughout slavery, and after, some of whom are passing as White. If the truth were told, the majority in America would be Blacks or African Americans, because slavery produced many mulattoes; some so fair that they married and lived their lives in a White world (negating any contact with their Black family members, what a huge burden to carry throughout one's life). In this author's opinion my family would always come first. If I am loved then my background or ethnicity should not matter. Love is supposedly blind, and it is in the eye of the beholder—well, maybe not.

One of the ways to tell if a Black is "passing" is that most of them will not have any children, or will say that they are unable to bear children. Therefore, these families opt for adoption. This, of course, means that they usually adopt a "white" child or two and now their family is complete (note: please know that in America if one has a "drop" of Black blood he/ she would be considered Black). There are however, some very beautiful mixed blue-eyed, blonde children who will one day have to choose their ethnic heritage, if America continues to "label" its citizens. I understand in recent years the mother has the duty to label her child whatever she considers the child to be. The need to be identified with one group or the other seems nonsensical. In the twenty-first century America should not need its labels and boxes. A few Whites in past years came up with more terminology and concepts including "let's allow Blacks to assimilate," by "melting" into White society. This "melting pot" theory has not been completely successful thus far. Assimilation then became pluralism (allowing members of other groups to enjoy and retain their culture while working and performing in the wider society). Today, the term is the "salad bowl," with diversity and multiculturalism, where all groups are to be celebrated and validated. It is unfortunate that America has to label all groups; and to consider color first in America! There should be only two boxes to check—Are you an American?—Or not? In which case, which country are you from? This author visited Paris, France and was greeted at the airport as an "American."

The destiny of all Black people is invariably connected to the future of the Black family. Black marriages need to be stable and to remain for the sake of the children. The out-of-wedlock practices by the youth needs to be stopped; the youth need to consider marriage first and children second. The Black community, in order to survive, needs to start its own economic institutions, as it has had in the past. These institutions would enrich and serve in a positive capacity that traditionally belonged to the Black community of old. Integration is fine, but it has not totally worked for all Blacks in America. And it has not been the "ticket out" that some Blacks had hoped it would be.

A few Black women have found it difficult to find a "good" Black man. Some have opted to become impregnated by artificial insemination or have resigned to the idea of just being in a relationship sans marriage. Many of these Black women who have made these choices are professional, middle-class women, with financial security who want children. Adoption is not an option for those who want their own children. Some Black women are also moving toward the women's liberation movement (or feminism—a movement in conjunction with White women to a certain extent). Still others are going back to the submissive, supportive roles held by Black women in years past.

More progressive Black "Sisters" have picked up some of the ways of African women to bring in some cultural elements to their families; for example Kwanzaa celebrations. Many people ask: (as mentioned previously) Why can't a Black woman find a "good Black man?" Here are some reasons:

- Incarcerated in either jail or prison
- Married outside their own group
- Already married in their group
- Homosexual
- Die young—drugs and alcohol related
- Drive by shootings
- Gang related
- Shortage of male babies
- Insufficient education

At the time of this writing, in 2011, many Black females are the heads of their households in greater numbers than comparative groups. More than ever, the extended family kinship system is needed within the African American communities. It was once seen as dysfunctional to have other members in a household, but for the Black family it was always functional and needed. According to Moyd:

> The next problem that affects the Black family is the welfare system. A percentage of Blacks, namely women who are single, divorced, or widowed with a child and without a male presence in the home rely on welfare for economic survival. The funny thing is males were not allowed to be part of a family if it was to receive welfare (sounds like another case of "slavery" time practices). Because of this prerequisite, many times Black men were forced to leave their families during hard economic times in order that his family could eat and survive. [6]

I believe that women should work if physically and mentally able. However, welfare in this author's opinion was/is just another form of slavery. Someone is always probing every aspect of the woman's life, and that is too much "control" to live under. The best alternative would be; to get an education and then a job. In many cases Black men could not get a job that would pay enough to take care of a family. The lack of employment was a direct way to keep the Black man subject to the role of "boy." Some of these concerned men made arrangements to camp with their peers by day and sleep with their families by night. Sadly, this simple survival technique did not last long. When the welfare agent found out, a cadre of night agents was organized whose only function was to spy out and to raid these Black homes (criminally breaking in if necessary) and catch these fathers sleeping with their families. This was the old way and has been continued until recent years. How horrible, even when families tried to stay together—it was not possible. The newspaper headlines would read, "Black Father Goes to Jail for Welfare Cheating", reporting the results of these raids in both Black and White newspapers. However, this was simply another ploy to disrupt the Black family. If the male could not find work, then he could not take care of his family. The real truth is that the majority of people on welfare are White, not Black.

While the majority of Black fathers cared for their children, some were unable to do very much because of low-paying jobs, but they did what they could. However, since the institution of marriage has been abandoned for several decades, the Black women are virtually "without a man" today. Some Black men seem to be playing outdated parts that are reminiscent of slavery. In other words, you father the child but you do not have any responsibility for its care. The state will supplement the mother and take care of your charges. This is not a positive mind-set, yet it is a notion that has filled the void in the Black family. Good, fatherly role models are very hard to find anymore for many Black families. This practice of not taking responsibility must stop.

Young people must become educated and self-sufficient. These chains of the past must be shed, and a new approach to life in America must spring forth. For Black men, looking for jobs that provide substantial compensation means acquiring a college education. High school diplomas are not enough. For many years, higher education was not available to Blacks, especially males. Even today, racism keeps many qualified Black men from employment and higher education. However, this was not the case for most Black women in America, especially in recent years. More Black women are highly educated and have meaningful positions in corporate offices throughout America.

Today the bondage is not the "chains" on the body, but the chains on the mind. This is a more difficult "chain" to break, and many of Willie Lynches' predictions unfortunately have held true within the Black community to this present day! Racism has again reared its "ugly head". There was a recent incident in Jena, Louisiana. A group of boys, White and Black, engaged in an altercation in 2006. The Whites had hung "nooses" on a tree called "The White Tree." Some Blacks sat under the tree, and the scuffle began. However, the White students were given a lenient sentence and the six Blacks were ordered to a harsher sentence totaling 100 years in prison. The Black students were tried as adults. Does this sound like 21st Century America? In 2007, after the news media gave attention to this matter, the six Black youths were released from prison.

In America there is always a call for the "world" to become democratic, and fair. Somehow this does not seem to be the way it really is in America. How dare America 'preach' to the rest of the world when America does not guarantee equality to all of its citizens. Blacks have come a long way; but unfortunately it seems we still have more issues to overcome. America, while attempting to finally overcome racial problems, is deficient as the struggle continues. This author knows that there is only one 'race' and that is the "human" race. We are all a part of the human family called Homo sapiens. There is no sub-variety of humans. If labels were necessary then 'ethnicity' would seem to be a more realistic term than the word 'race.' However, the plight of Black males continues.

More and more, Black men are not around long enough to build a marriage or a strong relationship with Black women. The biggest culprit of this crime is a society that has locked the Black male out of the mainstream through a pattern of bias actions. This is seemingly a throwback to slavery, where the males were made to sire children and the master would sell them for a profit. There was no paternal connection then, and, it seems, for whatever reason there are not many paternal connections today in far too many cases. A Black male cannot commit to a family when he has no job, or no chance of getting one because of a prior record (jail or prison). For many African American men, there has not been much hope of being completely successful; the situation seems almost to be by design. The new migration seems to be that many young male Blacks are incarcerated; still missing from their families.

The "Great Migration" coincided with an explosion of mechanized and industrial manufacturing in the south. Black male power was largely not needed in the south; there were only a few older men and boys left to work at home with the mother and/or the grandmother. When a job was secured by the husband then the rest of the family would be sent for later. As mentioned previously, the north had its share of problems with something called "Jim Crow." These were restrictive laws that were meant to keep Blacks in their place. This included housing, jobs, and low salaries.

Blacks faced a new set of obstacles in the north, though they were not as blatant as they had been in the south. Black men were finally able to work and began to care for their families. Various communities were formed as each ethnic group joined together to help one another. These little ethnic communities were known for a specialty; food, clothing, or jewelry for example. This came very close to pluralism in its best form. Some of these group members worked outside their community but still spent their money and their time within their specified communities. Before integration, Black professional people who had worked very hard and received an extensive education headed most of the Black families. These Black families served as examples to other Black families in the communities and throughout the nation to inspire them. Many families strived to achieve the American dream. Most of these positive examples were lost in the integration process because

Black people moved from the old neighborhoods and lost the sense of community. It was vital during segregation for Blacks to own their own businesses and to have their own professional providers. These people were the "role-models;" Blacks depended upon themselves, not outsiders. Black people were achievers and hard workers; some of that seems to have been lost in recent years because of integration.

Blacks contributed greatly to America and the world and all Americans should be thankful for them. However, the inter-relationships between Black men and women have seemingly changed in the past forty years. The strong family bonds that once existed now seem to be in decline. The search for wealth and riches has caused many Black people to lose their perspective on the value of life and the importance of raising a productive family. Fortunately, this has only been a small fraction of the African American or Black group. However, the majority of Black families seem to believe the notion that their children will achieve much more than they were able to. Each generation tends to hope for a better tomorrow for their children. The positive changes must come and come soon. The time for change is now. For a people to survive there needs to be fluid dynamic change, as nothing ever remains static. We live in an ever-changing world. If the Black family is to survive, then it is vital to find positive ways of keeping the family unit intact. Black families constitute an important segment of social life in America. According to Macionis:

> In 1996, Black families were made up of 46 percent female-headed families and male-headed families made up 7%. In 1996 the typical African American family earned $26,522, only 63% of the national standard. People of African ancestry are also three times as likely as whites to be poor, and poverty means that families experience unemployment, underemployment, and, in some cases, a physical environment replete with crime and drug abuse. [7]

This was and is a serious obstacle especially for Black families. They need fathers to provide positive role model behavior. Meaning simply, that the man needs to be the "head" of the household, he needs to work, and to provide for his family. He should be tender and loving to his wife and children. These examples will show the young boys how a "real" man behaves and provides for his family.

However, the significance of Black families lies not in numbers, but in the crucial role Blacks have played in the evolution of world history and in American society. This happened, in spite of the problems that Blacks had been struggling under. Therefore, with a concerted effort to solidify and strengthen the family; Blacks would have much more to offer their communities and the broader society. Blacks need to pick up the mantle and meet the challenge by writing, researching, and studying to have their proper place in American history. In recent years there have been positive studies written by Blacks and others with a realistic and sincere effort to counteract the negative images that have been written from the past. The Black family has sustained itself throughout the horrors of slavery and reconstruction; from the late 1800s, down through the years until the present. It is hoped and prayed that the family will remain a viable force in the lives of African Americans. The family, marriage and the church are the main foundations that African Americans can hold on to in America. These three institutions are major segments of sociological theory and practice. And, these three institutions from God (marriage, family and the church specifically) must be preserved if the Black group is to survive with dignity and a true sense of pride as we march proudly further into the 21st century!

In the World ye shall have tribulations: but be of good cheer; I have overcome the world.
(John 16:33)

Chapter VII.

The Black Church—The Black Religion

African American religion did not just come about when Africans were reintroduced to the New World. Christianity began in the area surrounding Africa. According to *The Original African Heritage Study Bible,* Ethiopia was the first Christian nation. Africans did not need Europeans to save their "souls." Africans were the original people and they knew God. However, through the period of hundreds of years, some Africans began to worship other gods and lost their original zest for the omnipresent God. This is similar to what happened to the children of Israel (the Jewish nation), when they turned from God. As an example, they struggled in slavery under the Egyptian Pharaoh for four hundred and thirty-two years; Africans in America suffered for nearly the same period of years under European dominance. Both groups suffered similar fates for their disobedience to God. God is no respecter of humankind. Ethiopia is mentioned in the Holy Bible over 45 times and Egypt is mentioned 155 times.

During slavery in America, Blacks were forced to attend church with their slave owners and they had to sneak around at night to practice their own religious beliefs. Throughout slavery there were a group of Blacks that would meet usually by the riverside to worship God. In order to better understand the Black religion in America we have

88

scholars who have provided research into the past, attempting to explain what Black people believed from ancient times to the present.

Most of the ensuing information will come directly from *The Original African Heritage Study Bible:*

> Christianity originated in Africa because God gave His creation His words and laws. Christians are of the group of God. This was prior to the birth of Jesus, His son, of whom Christianity was officially named many thousands of years later. The people were first called Christians in a city called Bethel, because they were followers of Christ. Psalm 68:31: Princes shall come out of Egypt; Ethiopia shall soon stretch out her hands unto God. [1]

It reminds this author of the moment when God sent Joseph, Mary and Jesus to Egypt because King Herod wanted the child killed. Think for a moment, if they looked European how could they have possibly hidden in Black Egypt? Europeans have been writing about how Egypt is a part of the Middle East or a part of southern Europe; it is not true; Egypt is still northern Africa!

According to *The Original African Heritage Study Bible* ("The Ancient Black Christians"):

> John Mark took his teachings of Christ into Egypt, but the original Christianity was already there. Keep in mind that the Garden of Eden was located in the Eastern section of Africa where the Tigris and Euphrates rivers intersect. John Mark was ordained the first bishop of Africa. By the year 189 A.D., Christianity appears to have been well established all across North Africa. Many Christians died in the persecution directed against them by other religious zealots like the Romans and Muslims. There were many religious wars and persecutions in history and yet Africa is mentioned in very few texts." [2]

Africa was a Christian nation as God was the Father of Adam and Eve. The Bible has many things that need to be explored, and understood. Also from *The Original African History Study Bible:*

> St. Maurice was a Black General in 287 A.D. He and his men be-
> came Christians while stationed in Africa. They were fervent be-
> lievers in God, and would not serve the pagan gods anymore.
> After his death in Europe, St. Maurice became highly revered in
> the Christian arena. [3]

St. Maurice was a revered statue in the Catholic faith. Africa had many early Christians and priests in the Catholic Church. Continuing *The Original Heritage Study Bible:*

> Finally, the edict of Milan, in about 300 A.D., was issued by the
> Roman state, granting social and political freedom to Christians.
> It was no longer a crime to practice the Christian faith. [4]

Surprisingly enough, Catholics were not considered to be Christian by most of the North African and Ethiopian congregations at that time in history. But then again, most of the Catholic "religious" holidays are also based upon holidays of "pagan" people; now converted Christians. Today, Christians practice these holidays out of tradition; recognized by the Catholic church; among those are Halloween, Easter, and Christmas. Most knowledgeable Christians realize this truth, and have attached a religious meaning for these holidays; therefore, aligning themselves with Catholic practices and belief systems. The exception is Halloween, which, for the most part, Protestants have left for Catholics to celebrate. Due to the edict of Milan, Christianity was now free to prosper and develop. The history of the African involvement in the early church continues with many sagas and contributions made by Africans.

It has been repeatedly stated that Christianity began in Africa, which was widespread prior to the European Christian era. By the beginning of the 4th Century, in Eastern Africa, Christianity had become the state religion of Ethiopia. In Roman Africa, St. Augustine had succeeded in spreading his Christian influence early in the 5th Century, and also to the known world at this time. Soon after, the Nubians of the Middle Nile and some of their neighbors to the south embraced the Christian faith. Although it seemed that most of Africa had accepted and embraced this religion, there were vast areas in Africa that did not want to deal with European Christian faith. They held on to their indigenous faiths. Similarly, the version of Christianity that was made popular in Europe, never achieved full dominance in Africa.

Africans did not wait for either the Muslims or the European Christians to provide a religious basis for their existence. For many centuries, Blacks had relied on their own special brand of theology and spirituality to explain the mysteries of the universe and their destiny as human beings. Africans always knew that there was one great God. Although in some tribes/clans they had beliefs in several lesser gods. There was a belief that great Africans of of the past; or the 'forefathers', were somehow able to help with the present and the future of some American Blacks through their worship practices. Now the path to Christianity was brutal in Europe. According to John G. Jackson in *Man, God, & Civilization*:

> The barbarians began to overrun the Western Roman Empire in the early part of the fifth century, and by the end of that century Roman civilization was in ruins. Europe then entered upon the long night of the Dark Ages, which lasted for five hundred years (500-1100 A.D.). The Dark Ages, as Professor Thompson truly said, "were at least as much due to the corruption of the church as to the decay of Roman civilization or… barbarian invasions." It was this period in history which chronicled many horrors; it was the beginning of Europe's conversion to Christianity. "Could the full history of the conversion of Europe to Christianity be written," said Dr. Briffault, "it would present a tale of horror more appalling than that of the Christianity of Spain during the Inquisition. [5]

The Christian religion had been imposed upon the people of Europe in much the same manner as it was imposed on Mexico and Peru. According to *The Original African Heritage Study Bible*:

> …De Las Casa estimates that twelve million died as most were butchered, tortured and burnt alive. De Casas was the head

priest of the Catholic church who gave the orders to take Africans into slavery in order to spare the Native Americans, or "Indians," in America. Some so-called "Christians" were the major perpetrators of the enslavement of Africans and other people of color throughout the world. [6]

It seems that the church will have much to answer to God concerning the treatment of humans in this world. Rogers wrote the use of Negroes came about thusly:

> Good Bishop Las Casas (1474-1566) seeing the Indians dying under the tasks imposed on them suggested the African instead—a step that has made Las Casas go down in history as the father of the African slave trade. He lived to regret it bitterly. He said in his old age that had he known its consequences, "he wouldn't have done it for the world." [7]

This means that no matter what the station in life, the position of a man of the cloth can conceivably do hateful and barbaric things to others all in the name of God. Perhaps because the church went along with slavery so did some Caucasian men—it was about finances. Slavery was an economic venture for the European. The church not only perpetuated slavery, but also created it where it had never existed under Roman law. No one could honestly say that America would not be the grand country that it is if it had not been for the African slave that built this country from nothing, by their blood, sweat and tears. Blacks were artisans, and skilled ironworkers. In fact, on the top of the Capitol in Washington, D.C., is the Statue of Freedom. A Negro slave erected the statue and placed it into position—his name was Phillip Reed. Have you ever heard this fact before? Probably not, as much of Black history has, in the words of Dr. Bill Cosby, been lost, strayed or stolen. Rogers continues:

> Planters would say, "Negroes are the lifeblood of the plantations. Without them we could not exist." Southern planters, quoting the Bible, called Africans "the one thing needful..." Everything is by God's blessing in good condition and in consequence of the employment of Negro slaves. [8]

In the 1960's many young African Americans believed that Christianity was only for Caucasians and not for people of 'color.' Many books had stated that slaves were 'a blessing from God.' However, as arrogant as that sounded, it was partially correct. God was avenging His chosen people the Israelites for their enslavement in Egypt for over four hundred years. We must remember that God is no respecter of persons. It seems to this author that Africans had to be in bondage also. We must note that both groups disobeyed God's laws, and worshipped other gods!

Blacks from Africa participated in many historic events, especially all of the wars starting with the Revolutionary War. However, the history books will not reveal these truths, as they have been virtually thrown out, and/or left out of the historical pages deliberately. Rogers wrote concerning Patrick Henry:

> He deplored "the necessity of holding his fellow-men in bondage." But that "their manumission is incompatible with the felicity of the country." Thomas Jefferson and a few other so-called humane slave owners said the same thing. [9]

It is fine to feel compassion, but ultimately they did nothing to have them released or to change the laws to help the enslaved—so they suffered just the same. Paul advised one slave, Onesimus, in the Holy Bible to return to his master because slaves should be obedient to their owners (God had commanded them to be slaves!) Again, this was because of Paul's knowledge that slaves were persons of worth and were not all to be treated poorly. In this case Paul knew Philemon, and had converted him into becoming a Christian. Paul's relationship with Philemon led him to believe that Onesimus was no longer considered a slave but now "a brother" as they were both Christians. This suggests all Christians should treat each other as "brothers and sisters".

As this author has stated, American slavery was one of the worst and harshest in recorded history after the so-called enlightened period of history. In the ancient period in history, slavery was 'the norm'.

It was a way of life from Biblical times throughout the 17th century. Mankind seems to have forgotten that all men had a common beginning. All people were from the one common human family (Adam and Eve)—God orchestrated creation. We must remember that when God stopped the people from building the Tower of Babel, He spread them to the four corners of the earth and confused their language. At that time prior to God stepping in, the people all spoke one common language, and they lived together. However, after the separation of the people there was no more harmony or getting along. Blacks were determined to achieve no matter what their circumstances. The Black churches grew and most are still active today. Daniel P. Seaton states from *The Original African Heritage Study Bible:*

> Because these Hamites were an important people, attempts have been made to rob them of their proper place in the catalogue of the races. The Bible tells us plainly that the Phoenicians were descendants of Canaan, the son of Ham, and anyone who will take the time to read the Bible account of their lineage must concede that fact. [10]

Some Bible scholars state that descendants of Ham were a cursed people and they were destined to be servants of their brothers. The above statement seems to dispel this myth. The following comes directly from *The Original African Heritage Study Bible,* Dr. Seaton continues:

> He was a prominent leader in the African Methodist Episcopal Church who wrote in 1895, displaying considerable knowledge about the Bible, the location of ancient religious sites, and the significance of many Biblical characters. In fact, he made several field trips to Palestine. In his major work a volume of 443 pages of text notes, maps, and illustrations, he provides extensive descriptions of tombs, villages, and other ancient sites, which he visited. It is noteworthy that Seaton's study displays a profound awareness of racism among the "bona fide" Bible scholars of his day. He could have benefited greatly from systematic, historical, critical engagement with the Biblical text in its original languages. [11]

However, racism in the church is not a new phenomena, it took "root" many years ago when it came to persons of color! We should remember that in Chapter 10 of Genesis, all the groups of the world are described as having been derived from one source and that was Noah and his family (descendants of Adam and Eve). According to the researchers of *The Original African Study Bible,* Noah is alluded to as indeed being a man of color. If, then, this information is factual, all of the present people on earth after the Flood had the same beginnings. African slaves brought with them to America the belief system called "African Traditional Religion." This support of one sacred power along with their spirituality helped slaves deal with life. Though the African continent is very large, it was divided into various countries each with its own culture, languages, dialects, and belief systems. Therefore, the African Traditional Religion's success in North America was not as great as in Latin America. The slaves attempted to communicate with each other by grunts and groans, and by showing one another hand signals similar to sign language to convey what they were trying to say. Each new batch of slaves had to be introduced to the form of communication that the slaves had among themselves. Some were able to keep alive in their hearts the old religious ways. When they were alone in the "dead of night," they would steal away; quietly down by the river to pray; mainly praying to God for their freedom. Remember that none of the Africans necessarily came from the same language groups or the same tribes. Therefore, they could not understand each other, but they could all understand the drums—they were universal. Seeing as the Europeans forbade the slaves to play the drums, the main commonality that the slaves shared was their stressful conditions and suffering created by this strange-looking "blue-eyed white-skinned creature." This could be cited as "cultural shock." Stressed daily by the pressures of slavery, the Africans' power for coping with enslavement (like believing that he had the ability to fly in order to avoid whippings or other abuses) is, perhaps what some psychologists would term or call the use of a form of mental power to survive. These and other methods were employed by some African slaves to help them in their dire moments of crisis.

Christianity, in its anti-slavery version presented a slave-hating God who controlled the universe and intended to liberate the slaves in His own good time. Christianity was no longer just a White religion in America: Slaves had discovered a form of Christianity with a friendly brown face. Blended with beliefs and mysteries of Africa, this was turned inward to form a state of wellbeing; bringing them a sense of power and comfort; to keep themselves sane while struggling in their horrendous situation. It is apparent that Christianity played a major part in the survival of the Black group in America. However, many older people remembered a different time, or their parents told them of how it used to be in their homeland Africa. Africa was remembered as the place of freedom and mysterious power. African American-born slaves tended to view native Africans as a people like themselves even though there were great variations in American Christianity based upon the European pattern of worship.

The Queen of England also endorsed slavery, as did all the powers that were—at that time the economic aspect of buying and selling humans was very profitable. However, the growth of Christianity among slaves did not exclude the memory of influences from Africa. For these Black Americans, Christianity provided the large perspective on life, death, and their very destiny, while the African heritage provided concrete ways of dealing with everyday problems relating to health, interpersonal relations and the natural world. Both the Christian and the African Traditional Religion were prevalent within the African American community. The Black church has historically been a stalwart and major supporter of the African American. The slave's form of religion most of the time served the master's interest, but for many slaves it fueled the resistance that shaped their religion. Slaves came to believe that their religion took on a greater force in respect of their humanity than did their masters' religions. Whether or not the slaves were able to resist openly, they could resist in their hearts, knowing that God intended for them to have freedom. There were many problems even for Blacks attempting to serve the Lord. The main reason for the denial of Blacks to congregate together was based on the fear of insurrection or plotting to run away. Further, if Blacks were taught brotherhood and equality for all mankind before God, they would not be content to remain in bondage. So it was necessary to lie to them and to remind them that God wanted them to be in servitude. "Servants obey your master, this is the will of God." Of course, this was added with other quotes out of context from the Bible. Even at that, slaves knew that God wanted them to be free. The White owners had to find a method to protect their rights to own slaves and to remain in positions of power over them. The masters would also tell Black preachers to reiterate the same types of sermons. To ensure that this was done, a White minister would be in the church to make sure no meaningful truth was spoken.

Slaves believed that Jesus was the Messiah-King who would liberate them, as Moses had liberated the Israelites. And, Jesus was also the Savior who would carry them to freedom in heaven. In the slaves' mind, the White man's religion was hopelessly corrupt, for it favored slave holding. The masters' hypocritical religion would not protect them from God's sure punishment. Meanwhile, the followers of God's true religion should live as God meant from the beginning. For many slaves, this meant a resistance as a Christian duty. This included flight, sabotage, malingering, or whatever the slave could do in regard to halt the progress on the plantation. The average slave day was from sunup to sundown, with maybe a day off on Sunday or at least part of Sunday off. According to Franklin & Moss:

> The invitation to Negroes to attend the white churches, the acceptance of which bordered on compulsion, did not represent a movement in the direction of increased brotherhood. Rather, it was a method that white employed to keep a closer eye on the slave. It was believed that too many of the conspiracies had been planned in religious gatherings and that such groups gave the abolitionist an opportunity to distribute incendiary ideas and literature. When Bishop Atkinson of North Carolina raised the question "Where are our Negroes," he not only implied that they were in churches other than the Episcopal church but that they were beyond the restraining influence of the conservative element of the white society. When the slaves attended the

churches of the planters; they usually sat either in the gallery or in a special section. The earliest examples of racial segregation are to be found in the churches. [12]

Such fears by slave-owners proved accurate, for many of the most obedient and influential slaves had a keen understanding of the difference between the gospel of pro-slavery preachers and the Christian scriptures' message of divine punishment for oppressors and liberation for the faithful. Christianity is a freedom-based religion. Now, exactly what should be done with all of the freed Blacks after 1863 and 1865? The early White Americans were faced with a very grave situation. Some wanted to send all Blacks back to Africa, and some Blacks wanted to return. However, most Blacks decided that they had been in America for so long and had built this country; they wanted to stay. They did not want to forget their relatives that had died in America.

Some Blacks participated in the "Back to Africa" movement, and there were several trips made to Africa from America at that time. Lincoln and others felt that it was the only thing to do. Since Blacks were no longer considered to be property, under White dominance, they had no further use in America. Unfortunately, this was not very successful, because few Blacks felt an alliance to Africa after being in America for hundreds of years. They had forgotten their languages and dialects. Most Whites wanted all Blacks to return to Africa to rid the country of their existence. Even though Blacks had been mal-treated by Whites, America was still the only home that they knew. On the other hand, Marcus Garvey was a strong advocate for the "Back to Africa" movement in the 1920s. He was a proud Jamaican and he owned ships that could be used to transport Blacks back to Africa. The sad truth is that some freed Blacks were not respectful to the native Africans they encountered. The Blacks that went back formed a new country in Africa that was called Liberia. The capitol was Monrovia, named after President James Monroe. It was just another colony of the United States. It was interesting to find that the Black Americans had the tendency to treat the native Africans similar to the way Whites had treated them in America (which merely means that was all they knew after so many years of being mistreated in America). Mistreatment for long periods of time becomes a virtual "way of life."

At the same time as some Blacks were leaving the country, the U.S. government was putting in place a program designed to assist newly freed Blacks and poor Whites. This was called the Freedmen's Bureau. This effort provided health and hospitals, built some schools, and many Blacks learned to read and write. The Bureau's aim was to negotiate fair wages for Blacks, but the program was short lived and ultimately did little to help many displaced and unemployed Blacks. Reconstruction was also a short lived project, the Federal Government withdrew the federal troops from the South and left White Southerners in charge of their lives and the lives of Blacks. They had the ability to decide what they wanted to do with the freed Blacks. The vote that was given to Blacks was quickly taken away. Many poll taxes and other blocks were put in place to keep Blacks from voting and from having a decent quality of life. Whites were determined to be superior and to remain in power. The various hate groups arose about this time, including the Klu Klux Klan. The Southerners also came up with Black Codes, which attempted to put most Blacks back into a form of slavery. This was to the dismay and horror of the newly freed Blacks who were left defenseless and at the mercy of their former masters. In spite of the abuse and poor treatment, this was home for countless Blacks and they refused to just get up and leave. It was a blessing that most Black fore parents decided to stay in America.

Blacks were determined to survive because of the sacrifices previously made by their forefathers. America was their country too, and they were determined to stay here. After all, many Black people had fought in every war, died for democracy, and yet, it eluded them back home in America. Remembering how this country was built from the blood and sweat of countless Black persons, Blacks had a right to be here and to be treated with equality and justice.

Again, the church was all that Blacks had to depend upon. The Black minister now no longer had to say what he was told by the overseer or the master. The White man was no longer directly in charge anymore. Blacks were free to worship God as they saw fit and it pleased them to worship in spirit and in truth, with a joyful noise and shouting "hallelujah!" The Bible was read and discussed as the preacher decided with the help of the Holy Ghost what was needed to benefit the members. Or as some ministers say today, "being led by the Spirit" or "the Holy Ghost." Today, there is a large difference between the services in predominately all-White churches and Black churches. And as stated earlier, ironically, it is a very segregated time in this so-called integrated nation. The White groups tried to work together at first to keep an eye on Blacks in their church procedures, which led to distrust.

There was not only the conflict between the progressives and the conservatives, but also a struggle between Whites and Blacks in general. In many localities Whites tried to control Black Baptist associations and conventions, much to the distress of the Black leaders. When Blacks were refused the privilege of participating in the management of the American Baptist Publication Society, under pressure from Southern churches, the organization refused to accept contributions from Blacks to obtain Sunday school literature. A serious breach then developed between the two groups. It was very sad that these two groups could not even agree on the fundamental beliefs that Blacks had a right to have ownership of their own churches and learning materials. This was down to undue interference by some White Christians. Franklin & Moss state:

> The white Methodists of New York had much the same attitude toward their Negro fellows, as did their counterparts in Philadelphia. The result was a withdrawal of Negroes from the John Street Methodist Episcopal Zion Church, and the establishment of the African Methodist Episcopal Zion Church in 1796. Leading in this movement were Peter Williams, James Varick, elected the first Bishop in 1822, George Collins and Christopher Rush. They could find no one in either the Episcopal or the Methodist church who would ordain and consecrate their elders, and finally they had to do it themselves. Overcoming schisms within and opposition without, the church was sufficiently stable

by 1822 to elect a bishop and to set up a program of expansion. The same trend toward independent organizations manifested itself among the Baptists. In 1809 thirteen Negro members of a white Baptist church in Philadelphia were dismissed to form a church of their own. Under the leadership of Reverend Burrows, a former slave, it became an important institution among the Negroes of that community. The Negro Baptists of Boston, under the leadership of Reverend Thomas Paul, organized their church in 1809. At about the same time, he was assisting in organizing the church in New York that later came to be known as the Abyssinian Baptist Church. In each instance organization was brought about as a result of the separation of blacks from white congregations. [13]

This author cannot fathom why any Blacks would want to be members of the Methodist or Baptist churches; rather than Quakers; considering all the abuse and maltreatment that came along with them. Franklin & Moss continue:

"Once the planters were convinced that conversion did not have the effect of emancipating their slaves, they sought to use the church as an agency for maintaining the institution of slavery. Ministers were encouraged to instruct the slaves along the lines of obedience and subservience. Bishops and high church officials were not above owning slaves and fostering the continuation of slavery....The Presbyterians and Quakers seemed to have been the most liberal in their attitude toward Negroes, but they were not the large slaveholders. The latter were to be found in the Episcopal Church on the Atlantic seaboard and in the Baptist and Methodist churches in the cotton kingdom. In the last three decades before the Civil War the church became one of the strongest allies of the pro slavery element. Slaves who had found refuge and solace in the religious instructions of the white clergy had reason to believe that an enemy that had once befriended them now trapped them. [14]

The so-called freedom promised to the slaves did not happen. In other words, whether you were Christian or not, slavery was going to remain. In fact the church was one of slavery's main supporters.

The major denominations that Blacks belonged to were/are the Baptist, Methodist, and The Church of God in Christ. The AME and AME Zion also tend to have had a large Black following in recent years. Remember, at one time it was reportedly said that if slaves became "Christian," then they would be given their freedom. Well, it did not take very long to see that this was just another "trick" by the White man. As thousands upon thousands of slaves were baptized, not many were treated any differently than before. Whites had stated that slaves would get special treatment, would be able to keep their families together, and have more time off. None of these things happened for the majority of slaves in America. There are always exceptions to any rule, and this case is no different. There were a few slaves, who upon accepting Christianity, survived better—but this was not true for the majority of slaves. Although church membership was increasing, organized religious bodies were going through a period that was as critical for Black as for Whites. Its leadership, however, was being effectively challenged by rising progressive elements, which refused to accept the crude notions of Biblical interpretation and the "grotesque vision of the hereafter" portrayed by the conservatives. Educated Negroes began to reject the church as the agency of salvation and turned their attention more and more to the immediate problems at hand. They demanded a change in management that would give them leadership more in keeping with their improved intellectual levels. Frequently, the progressives withdrew from Baptist and Methodist denominations and joined with Congregational, Presbyterian, Episcopalian, and Catholic churches, some of which seemed to have had more flexible attitudes toward the reforms on which the progressives insisted.

The first in a movement away from "traditional" Black churches was the Black Muslims in the 1950s and early 1960s. The Black Muslims were a sect based loosely on the Mohammedan faith and advocating strict separation of the races. Prior to the 1960s the words Black or Negro implied: dirty, soiled or stained with dirt, without moral goodness; whereas the meanings of White or Caucasian implied: innocent, pure as the driven snow, morally pure, innocent. This was the manner in which these terms were listed in the dictionary of old. No wonder no one wanted to be called Black; the words were always considered to be negative. The terminology for White was always so positive. But, who wrote the dictionaries? When reality hit, and the publishers were enlightened then the wording was a bit more palatable for both groups. All of a sudden it was time for Black Pride. This was the period of time when James Brown was singing, "I'm Black and I'm Proud." Prior to the new burst of Blackness, it was difficult for some Blacks to even want to be called Black because of the connotations associated with being Black in America. For verification take a look at an old dictionary and read what Black meant, or Negro, compared to White or Caucasian and their descriptions.

Other movements went back to the ancient African tribal religions that held sacred many gods in nature. However, even with these beliefs, they always knew and believed in the one almighty God. With the idea of 'Black consciousness' popularized through music, some of the traditional Christian denomination leaders began speaking out for a change. It was necessary; if Dr. King had remained silent concerning the "unjust laws" the progress that was gained towards equality would never have been started. Interestingly, many of the clergy felt that Dr. King being a minister of God was out of place working for the Civil Rights movement. Who was more qualified to be concerned? Men of God have made many changes in history. It is ironic that Christianity was used to "keep Blacks under control during slavery;" and for many years following slavery. All of these hundreds of years, Blacks suffered under the guise of following the word of the Lord; which was being misinterpreted and often used to keep Blacks servile and in bondage. What a conflict? This author believes that this is why so many young Blacks converted to Islam in the 1960s.

In recent years, there have been ministers, such as Cone and Cleage who have studied and researched Black History as it relates to the Holy Bible. They have established what is called a 'Black Theology'. This is one of the latest in a set of religious directions for "modern-day" Blacks in America. Not all Blacks subscribe to Cone and Cleage but they have a right to their beliefs and this is why they are included in this book. In fact, Minister Cleage calls his church the Church of the Black Madonna:

> In the chapel area, instead of the traditionally stained-glass window, there is a large portrait of the Black Madonna and child painted very Black, with distinct Negroid features. This is quite startling for many people, both Black and White, who have never seen the usual paintings of these figures in anything but 'White.' [14]

In 1986, this author went to Paris, France and saw the statue of the Black Madonna and Child and took a picture of the statue. In some countries in Europe, the churches have many dark figures of Christ, his mother Mary, and the nativity scenes. America had most religious artifacts painted white instead of black, as was common practice historically.

Ultimately, religion has become an expression and celebration. This interpreted religion offers hope for a better life and future for the children. Man was created in the beginning in God's own image and likeness. The promise was to accept His son and then look forward to being with God for eternity (this is what some Europeans did to God; they made Him white). The original brown/black God was given European features and therefore their God looked very much like the persons who painted him, thereby personalizing their white God. Some other ideas according to Cone are as follows:

> This means that to love black people, he has taken on black oppressed existence becoming one of us. He (Jesus) is black because he loves us; and he loves us because we are black. [15]

These sentiments have been seen as reverse racism; however, this author maintains that a people without wealth, power or prestige, cannot be racist! In other words—some words may be harsh, but there are no consequences that Blacks can levy upon Whites in America to make a difference in their lives. As a collective group some Blacks may be wealthy, but it is sparse. There is no real power or prestige within the Black community to wield against Whites in any form. In other words Blacks can do nothing to withhold employment, housing or anything that really matters for a people to survive. Without wealth, power, or prestige no one group can harm any other group. Blacks may talk and feel aggressive but it is mostly talk. And that is a very good thing to be able to express oneself and share opinions. This is very healthy.

Many people will have a very hard time aligning themselves with such drastic statements made by Cone, but yet, many other ministers agree that these measures were necessary in order to counteract the oppression of "White racism," even as it relates to Christianity. These ministers think that all churches should adhere to their philosophy or belief system. This theology has been considered to be radical by many Blacks. Mainly Black Muslims and some of their teachings have utilized the following for these ideas. They further think that Black people must realize that a White Jesus' picture has no place in the Black community. Blacks should replace Him with a Black Messiah, as Albert Cleage would say (this author realizes that not all people, Black or White, will agree with Cleage):

> Unfortunately, American White theology has not been involved in the struggle for Black Liberation... and neither have all Black Americans. White oppressors or White theology has given re-ligious sanction to the genocide of Indians (Native Americans) and the enslavement of Black people... [16]

The churches had sanctioned slavery because it was profitable for the planters and the clergy—many of them owned slaves and reaped the benefits. According to Cleage:

> From the very beginning to the present day, American White theological thought has been "patriotic," either by defining the theological task independently of Black suffering (the liberal northern approach) or by defining Christianity as compatible with White racism) the conservative southern approach, that is. In both cases, theology becomes a servant of the state, and that can only mean death to black people. It is little wonder they conclude that an increasing number of young blacks are finding it difficult to be black and also to be identified with traditional theological thought forms of 'traditional Christianity.' [17]

The mistreatment by the clergy lends credence to the feelings of many Black males in the 1960s that perhaps God was for the White man and not for people of color.

Since the early 1960s, this has been a dilemma for some Black young people—what to believe in and what is true? Why do images of God not reflect a man of color? Blacks in the 1960s and 1970s were looking for answers and they were not able to accept the traditional, old and weary answers from the previous generations. Older Blacks were seen as "Uncle Toms, too old-fashioned, not being with 'what is happening'". This author notes, if the God of the Holy Bible was good enough for my ancestors He is good enough for me! Young Blacks wanted to try something new, and Black theology was that "something" for many Black people. According to James Cone:

> There are two reasons why Black theology is a Christian theology and possibly the only expression of Christian theology in America. First, there can be no theology of the gospel which does not arise from an oppressed community. This is so because God in Christ has revealed himself as a God whose righteousness is inseparable from the weak and helpless in human society. The goal of Black theology is to interpret God's activity as he is related to the oppressed Black community. [18]

This author's opinion is that Jesus had compassion upon the poor and the downtrodden, no matter what their ethnic group or color. Cone comments further:

> Black theology is Christian theology because it centers on Jesus Christ. There can be no Christian theology that does not have Jesus Christ as its point of departure. Though Black theology affirms the Black condition as the primary reality, which must be dealt with, this does not mean that it denies the absolute revelation of God in Jesus Christ. Rather it affirms it. Unlike White theology that tends to make the Christ-event an abstract, intellectual idea, Black theology believes that the Black community itself is precisely where Christ is at work. Most Blacks would like

to believe that this is true, as many lives in America are besieged
with problems stemming from an unjust system. [19]

It is hoped that eventually White and Black Americans alike will
be convinced that American Blacks have an historical background.
And they have made sufficient contributions to the development of
the human race, and have participated in the findings and in the origi-
nation of the birthplace of all of mankind. These roots are in the Holy
Bible.

It has been only in the past 25 years that Black scholars and ministers have made major breakthroughs on the subject that has been
ignored or suppressed by White religious authorities throughout modern history. Most of the modern research, however, is based upon the
findings of other Black historians like William Leo Hansberry and W.E.B.
Dubois, who identified major Black Biblical characters more than 50
years ago. Only a few persons listened to them, and now many researchers, historians, and ministers have validated the former information, using the Holy Bible as a book that God has written as a "map" for
His followers. There can be little doubt, of course, that the Caucasian
group implemented and made major "psychological" transformations
on Blacks; during and after slavery. Some Whites thoroughly convinced Blacks that they were inferior, no good, shiftless, and lazy. After
years of this type of negativity it became ingrained into the mind of
the person. It took years to behave in a negative manner and it will
take time to begin to behave in a positive manner. In spite of the information to the contrary, actually, Blacks built this country with their
blood, sweat, and tears from too many years of strenuous work under
horrendous conditions.

However, once a people buy into stereotypes, they begin to in-
ternalize them, and then it is very difficult to turn this self-negativi-
ty into something positive. It must be understood that it took many
years for Blacks to get the second-class "mind set," and it will take the
same amount of time, or more, for the truth to bring about the needed change. Some of the fastest growing churches were the Baptists,

Presbyterians, and the Quakers. After the Civil War, the Catholic churches, along with the AME and the AME Zion churches, began to grow
with larger numbers of Blacks as members. Please know that major
churches did little or nothing to stop slavery. Sure, there were always
a few ministers that would speak out, but their voices were often not
heard. Except for the few White ministers, for example John Wesley.
In fact, some ministers reaped benefits because their parishioners
were able to pay more money into the church if they had lots of slaves.
There was only one church that did many things to help slaves and
that was the Quakers, or the Friends church. It amazes this author as to
why most Blacks are not Quakers. Perhaps that is because most Blacks
are not cognizant of the true history concerning the Quaker churches
and their major contributions for the freedom of slaves.

One of the major forces that kept slaves going and gave them a
will to try to live was a form of religion better known in the Black community as "spirituality." Now we will examine three frequently used
terms: Spirituality, Christianity, and religion as defined in *Webster's
Dictionary*: Spirituality: Something that is an ecclesiastical law that be-
longs to the church or to a cleric as such. Christianity: As the religion
derived from Jesus Christ, based on the Bible as sacred scripture, and
professed by Eastern, Roman Catholic and Protestant bodies. Religion:
The service and worship of God or the supernatural. Commitment or
devotion to religious faith or observance. A personal set or institution-
alized system of religious attitudes, beliefs, and practices.

Black religions often embrace spirituality—and it is essential.
Some Blacks tend to be 'in touch,' if you will, with the higher power—God! This spirituality or communication with God can be done
prior to sleeping, while driving in one's car, or when one is at work.
In fact, this communication between God and man can happen any-
where and anytime, not just in a church building. To be exact, this is
the foundational root for the church and the mind-set of the Black
American. Without this concept of spirituality there would be no true
religious meaning for most Black Americans. This is the main basis for
the particular form of religious expression that can be found in African

American churches throughout the United States. As a matter of fact, most Black churches tend to be "louder" than other churches; because of the methods of worshiping and praising The Lord Jesus Christ. Some are more pronounced than others, but spirituality is the foundation of the Black belief system.

In the 1970s, approximately 18 million Blacks belonged to various Christian denominations in the United States. However, in an effort to clearly show their growing movement into spiritual realms, some Blacks moved away from the traditional religions that were symbolized by a White Mother and child. As stated before, one such movement was the Black Muslims. Another movement went back to the ancient African tribal religions that worshiped many sacred gods in nature. But the majority of Africans believed not in polytheistic forms of worship, but rather in a monotheistic God. Even the worshipers of many gods knew and believed in the One Supreme God. Within the traditional Christian denominations there were religious leaders speaking out for a change. This change needs to be shifted to include Black spirituality, and to realize that God is of color— that the Black man was shaped and formed in God's own image.

Many Black church leaders reveal a firm commitment to a common societal vision; namely a society that acknowledges as significant neither race, color, nationality, class nor station. Many have been unaware that their vision has been identical to the so-called melting pot theory that has been implicit in American consciousness both as fact and norm throughout much of the twentieth century. However, as my brother previously mentioned Sunday remains separate and segregated at 11:00 am. Also as mentioned earlier there has been some mingling of the various groups, especially African Americans and Caucasians attending integrated churches, but again this pattern is not largely seen in most cities throughout America. No matter how many laws are passed there are people who are still going to judge by the color of the skin, rather than as Dr. King so eloquently stated, by the character of a person. According to Paris:

Recently many sociologists, Black and White, have abandoned the melting-pot theory in favor of various theories of cultural pluralism, thus setting the terms of the present debate. The assimilations implied by the melting-pot theory aim towards an homogeneous culture, the full realization of which is thought by some to be impossible as long as a visible, racial factor is present. Theories of cultural pluralism, on the other hand, emphasize the importance of inclusion while affirming various differences of race, ethnicity, and religion. [21]

Cultural pluralism has been seen as the best of all theories to date. It provides for inclusion and also acknowledges the various ethnicities and their religions that may be present. Up to now man has decided which people are important on earth and which ones are not, as this book has attempted to point out by the many examples given. Hopefully, soon the term 'race' will be completely removed. Different-looking humans are what makes America the beautiful patchwork quilt that she is.

The term 'human' is a combination of two words; most people never take the time to consider the meanings of the words that we use, but as explained by Anthony Browder:

The term human can be divided into two basic words, hue and man. This literally means "man from the humus" (soil, the earth), a fancy way of saying Black man or man of color (hue), which describes the kind of man that evolved into human. [22]

Browder is correct with his interpretation of the word human. Evidentially, this portion of the word human (hue) relates to color—from ebony to ivory. Browder continues with information about color:

Basic genetics states that all colors are contained within melanin (or dark cells) and white cells contain no color. Simply put, it is possible for a race of brown, yellow, and white people to be produced from the cells of black people. But it is impossible for a race of black people to be produced from the cells of brown, yellow, or white races of people. [23]

It would seem that if any group evolved then it was the "fairer" group according to Browder. It would seem that black is the original and all other groups came from the one group. Browder further states:

All the early references speak of man as coming from the earth. Adam, the Biblical first man, is a word which means "man of the earth." The original name for Egypt was Kemit, which means "people of the Black land." The ancient Kemitian word Africa literally meant the "birthplace" of humanity. [24]

If the Bible for instance had been translated correctly the first time, then it would not be necessary to have had to go back and find the correct words and their meanings to bring out a balanced version, such as *The Original African Heritage Study Bible*. They had many talented researchers and historians of all "races"; who have helped to show the truth as it is being revealed. According to the Cress Theory:

What then necessitated changing the image of Black Jesus and Black Mary to White Christ and Mary? To answer this question, we must return to the most fundamental fact in the existence of the global white collective: White skinned people initially were the mutant albino of Black people in Africa. These White-skinned people were recognized as having a disease, just as today's modern science of genetics refers to the conditions of albinism (the lack of pigmentation) as a genetic deficiency disease. The pigmented population shunned the albinos or the fairer skinned people they banded together. The lighter skinned people were banned from living among the pigmentation group. This theory is just about as reliable as any in written history. When a group is given a chance to write their own history, this kind of information will be forthcoming. Europeans for the most part wrote history and it certainly identified their heritage and their "so-called" beginnings. [25]

This theory seems to have merit if indeed all colors evolved from black. According to Cress:

Eventually, they (light skinned people) had to migrate northward to remove themselves from the intense African sun rays. Migrating northward from Africa, the albino populations eventually settled in the area of the world now referred to as Europe. There, they increased in number and eventually returned to conquer the people of color in Africa, Asia, and the rest of the world. They returned with the idea that they would conquer and no longer think of themselves as the rejected and diseased population; instead, they would think of themselves, in compensation, as the superior and supreme supermen and look upon all skin-pigmented peoples as the 'genetic inferiors.' [26]

The "lacking," or the group without color, was jealous and perhaps felt inferior, and it seems that often the "lighter" group members were ostracized from the other groups of color. That could have been a cause for hostility. Cress states further:

> With the necessity for such a compensatory ideology and concept of self as superior, the White psyche could tolerate no concept of anything higher than the White self—not even God. Thus, when the concept of the Son of God was formulated, in their thinking, the "Son" eventually took the form of a White man, which by brain computer logic would mean that God himself had to be a White man. Thus, the White collective, in logical reality, is not worshiping any force beyond itself. [27]

If Whites had treated others with respect perhaps we would not have such a dilemma. Cress continues with her examination of the White collective psyche:

> Further, it is apparent that the collective White psyche felt anger towards God for bequeathing them with what is now understood as a genetic defect, namely white skin. In turn, they have spawned the thinking that doubts and denies the existence of God. Thus, they have conceived of themselves as being at war with nature, which is the reflection of God. They function as though they are in contest with God and try to out-create God. [28]

It would seem that if any group should be angry it would be the group "left out of the mix" so to speak. If Whites are indeed angry with God that might be the reason for so much bloodshed and killing of innocent people. By being aggressive and dominant they figured out how to be a form of god themselves! In the years following the reformation, Europeans pictured the Bible characters as being European. In the early days of the Bible period, there was no concern about color prejudice. It seems that most people were of color to one degree or another. In the newly translated version of the Holy bible we can see a deletion of the prior messages of negativity that had been given to Blacks for over four hundred years. It will take time for some people to understand, but for others it will be a revelation that has been long overdue.

All Christians can be thankful to the contributors of *The Original African Heritage Study Bible* for their great contribution to knowledge and the research of the truth. The contributors were a combination of ethnic groups. Each one researched their information and recorded the facts they discovered. We must remember that our God has no respect for one group; except of course, the children of Israel. It is wonderful to know that God is not a respecter of persons; He loves His entire "rainbow" of children equally and has prepared a place for each one of us that believe and trust in Him. This world is not our home and one day we will each leave this earth with nothing. That is the way we entered and that is precisely the way we will leave it! The only things in life worth having are the things we did for others. The Bible says what we do for the least of these we do unto The Lord Jesus Christ!

The below image is called "The Black Madonna of Częstochowa" (origin and date unknown). The Black Madonna is incredibly popular throughout the world. France has more Black virgins than any other country, and people worship her on every continent. This is important because most of the world has no problem honoring a Black virgin statue, and she is welcome. Surprisingly, some Americans also honor her, which is probably because many Americans came from other countries around the world and brought their religious icons and beliefs with them. This is what makes America so great; we have freedom of religion for all people. Now we need to end the last vestiges of "color consciousness" in America!

I will lift up mine eyes unto the hills, from whence cometh my help.
(Psalms 121:1)

The Conclusion

The information in this book has been researched over many years. It is hoped that this study will broaden the vision of some, pique the curiosity of others, and inform all about the many discoveries and explorations that Black Americans and their ancestors have made to early civilization. This study has taken the reader on a journey from the creation of humankind up to the present time period. This author could not have written this book without including a dedication to my Lord and Savior Jesus Christ. Without His birth and His life I would not have been able to complete this book or have the patience to work on it for several years. All thanks and praises go to Him—my everything.

This book was written primarily because of Chapter III, Civilization in Africa. If you re-read it perhaps you will feel the passion behind the words and understand this particular subject was the main force of my endeavor. This author has found "nuggets" in many places but they needed to be put all together. It took years of research to find out all that has been written about the African input to our world.

This author is further grateful to Joel Augustus Rogers, Lerone Bennett Jr., Ivan Van Sertima, Dr. Leo Wiener, Dr's. L.S.B. Leakey and wife Mary for their many contributions to make sure that this valuable information was passed on and not lost. There are too many authors to list them all here, but they have also made deep impressions on the intellect of the astute reader.

Importantly, this book was not intended to put other groups down or to say that Blacks are better than others. It was to show that because of racism and deception, the African/Black contribution has been left out of the history books and denied in the Bible. But, God, in His infinite wisdom, would not allow some Europeans to fully negate the Black presence in the scriptures or in history.

The "people of color" today, who now call themselves either Black or African American, have made major differences. It is about time that Blacks were able to label themselves. It is also imperative that the real history be told—that Africans and African Americans have contributed greatly to the world since the very beginnings of civilization. Africans were inventors, scientists, mathematicians, scholars, ministers and teachers, in the past and present. A few Greeks wrote about the "gifts" of the Africans, among those according to John G. Jackson were Herodotus, Diodorus, Strabo, Pliny,and Homer. Van Sertima wrote about the University of Timbuktu, among others, which had many great scholars, including doctors, judges and priests. It seems that the Greeks were determined to write about what they had learned over the years from Africa; however they took full credit for the Africans' accomplishments. For many readers, this book will be very hard to digest, but for others it will be "a marvelous revelation." With God's grace, it is hoped that each man will learn to live in peace and harmony with his fellowman regardless of race, creed, or religious beliefs. This obligation to love each person holds especially true for all Christians on earth. We must remember these motivational words from the scriptures: And ye shall know the truth, and the truth shall make you free. This author went on the Internet to glean additional information on "Race." This information is taken from the 2000 Census Definitions. White: People having origins in any of the original peoples of Europe, the Middle East, or North Africa. Black or African American: People having origins in any of the Black racial groups of Africa. American Indian and Alaska Native: People having origins in any of the original people of North and South America (including Central America), and who maintain tribal affiliation or community attachment. Asian: People having origins in any of the original peoples of the Far East, Southeast Asia, or the Indian subcontinent. Native Hawaiian and Other Pacific Islander: People having origins in any of the original peoples of Hawaii, Guam, Samoa,or other Pacific Islands. These "racial" categories were established for the U.S. Census Bureau by the Office of Management and Budget in October 1999. Note: Latino or Hispanic people are now considered to be an "ethnic" group rather than a racial group.

People coming from Mexico and/or the Southwest section of the United States are not classified as a "racial" group. This author believes it is too bad that the other categories are not classified as simply "humans". In the twenty-first century, African or Black Americans are refusing to be devalued, dehumanized and ignored. This author would like to make a direct challenge, especially to the parents of Black youth, to teach them about The Lord Jesus Christ. Then teach Godly values and morals in your home, by example. Remind your children about the need for excellence in education. And, be sure that they are taught about Black history, whether in a private setting or at school. This is a prerequisite for them to become all that they are capable of becoming. Black youth need guidance and support along with lots of love and understanding. The many discoveries and inventions made by Blacks in Africa and in America have given many needed implements for survival to all men throughout the world. The world owes a great debt of gratitude to the Black man.

Blacks must reject the notion of being "cool" and all of the "street jive," which includes some of the negative "rap songs." Many of these songs are demeaning to Black women, being called out of their names, and being put down, portraying them as 'hookers, sluts, and whores.' All of these young men and women had a mother. Surely they would not want anyone to say these type of words about or around their loved ones, be it mother, sister or other female family members. Another main ingredient is the need to attend church together, and remember the Creator always!

The Legacy will hopefully have answered many of the questions that have not been previously answered in other books or in school.

"Looking back while moving forward" seemed to be the ideal title for this book. It is also hoped that this will be a "bridge from the past to the present" and will not be seen as a negative journey, but a positive one. This author is deeply indebted to the contributor's of *The Original African Heritage Bible*.

We all need to thank God for His goodness and His protection that has enabled African Americans/Blacks to survive. May all who read this book appreciate the knowledge and the contributions they have made throughout the years; but neither let us not forget our White brothers and our Latino brothers who have written about Africans and the people who are now known as African Americans. Blacks desperately need to eliminate the negatives and focus upon the positives in life. May this "new" directional journey of enlightenment prevail as we, as a Christian nation, move forward together into the future!

Note: This book was not completed until after the election of 2009, and America elected the first African American. The election of President Obama is a history-making event. President Obama's speech on 28 August 2008 was exactly 45 years after Dr. Martin Luther King, Jr. spoke in Washington, D.C. Dr. King had "a dream." It took years, but in this author's lifetime the dream has come to fruition! To God be the glory, all things in due season will come to pass. This historic event will be forever engraved into American history, and it will prove that Americans can unite and work together regardless of skin tone or background. It will not matter as to how much he accomplishes, the "financial woes" were left to him by the previous president. The emphasis in his campaign message was unity and with that as a focus Americans should all benefit from his presidency. This author just could not imagine the many bigots from the past that are "turning over in their graves" as a result of America voting for a Black man. I wish it were possible to let them visit for a brief period of time to see into this century. God is good and He is good all of the time. White racists are looking forward to more members, especially when our economy is going down. When the economy suffers the Klu Klux Klan tends to grow because some Whites did not vote for, nor did they want, a person of color to be president of these United States. When times get hard in America then the vicious and wanton come looking for blood from people of color. Some people are "scared to death" because America now has a person of color running this country. Yet, there is only so much that the president can do. It takes the Congress and the Senate to help pass or deny bills and other legislature.

The Obama Family

This new family in Washington, D.C. is the most popular family in America bar none. There are children once again in the White House. Similar to President Kennedy and his family. America will never again be the same; this is a "new millennium," one that has never been seen before. Threats made to President Obama have been more numerous than to any prior president. The plot to kill him was uncovered by the police and the two main subjects have been arrested. This is a daily problem for the Secret Service who must be vigilant day and night to protect our president's life. Christians united we must pray for our president. Americans are of the belief that all is fine as far as race relations are concerned. The astute person will realize that the problem remains. Yes, even President Obama is aware of the problems that still persist in America. There have been so many death threats on his life, but the secret service is attempting to keep that a private matter. President Obama shattered the picture of a White male always being elected president however; there is still much work to be done in America. There has been tremendous progress over the years, but we have much to accomplish. Yet, we must be grateful for the progress made. Most Americans are still proud to stand up and say yes, I am an American. My prayers and hopefully the prayers of the entire nation will enable our new president to be outstanding, just and fair with all groups. He is a prime example of a multicultural person, and I thank God for that fact. Most Americans today are also multi-combinations of two or three ethnic groups. It should not be of any importance; the major concept is that we are all human!

Mrs. Michelle Obama is a lovely first lady, and so very elegant. When I saw her beside the Queen of England, I thought to myself she is also a queen! Then the two embraced, my tears began to roll. How I wish the world could embrace and solve all of our pressing problems. Thanks to Mrs. Robinson there is a wonderful grandma in the home for the Obama's two girls. They are truly blessed to have a mother and a father and also a grandmother in the home. As Americans we need to embrace our new president and what he is attempting to do for our country. America may not be aware of the prestige that is now growing for America in the world because of the new first family. Hopefully the American image will change in the world as a result of President Barack Obama! Thanks to the many skilled and knowledgeable authors of today we have a preponderance of materials to use that describe all of the historical events of recent months. Being grateful for all of the wonderful things that are going on in America today there is not much time left for exclusion—these are the days for inclusion of all Americans.

The Legacy begins with God the Father saying to Jesus Christ, let us make man in our own image and likeness. God took a lump of dust from the earth and breathed into the nostrils the breath of life. Mankind was made into a living creature. God then made woman from a rib from Adam's side. God saw that it was good. These two people populated the world at that time. Then came Noah and his family (descendants of Adam and Eve). The earth was filled with sin and wickedness continually, God was tired of it. This man Noah and his family, only did God save from the impending disaster that was to come upon the earth.

Noah and his family populated the earth and later Nimrod decided he didn't need God. He was going to find his way into heaven his way. He gathered workers and had them pile brick upon brick creating a tall tower. One day God noticed the tower and decided something had to be done to stop Nimrod. God and His son went down to earth and He changed the language and the brick maker did not understand the maker, and the building stopped. After God changed the language He separated the land and divided it so that the groups that understood each other bunched together and thus was the beginning of different language and cultures.

Now *The Legacy* continues: Africans were traveling, trading, and settling in new lands and leaving their particular influence on the native people there. Often these groups mated and had offspring, continuing the cycle of human kind. Some of the travel included walking, going by raft, or boat. The replicas of their rafts are still found in some of the islands. Thor Hyderdal duplicated the raft making techniques in 1969; he was very successful in taking his raft from western Africa to the Americas. This done to prove once and for all that Africans did traverse the Atlantic Ocean. Africans made an indelible mark on Mexico as the heads of the gods are still in Mexico to this day. Mexicans made sacrifices to the god Ilixton. He had a large head with kinky-looking hair a broad nose and large lips. The characteristics were strictly African (notice the front cover).

The Legacy continues: The civilization in Africa or nearby areas. Ancient Africans began to dominate their environment and to invent tools and methods of iron smelting. They ventured far and wide across the Oceans and visited many places throughout the world. They even came as far as America according to Dr. Leo Wiener, Thor Hyderdal,Ivan Van Sertima, Lerone Bennett, and Dr. J.A. Rogers.

The Legacy continues on the subject of the sociological significance of race and ethnicity: This is important because sociologists do not believe that race is a major factor as it relates to the various groups throughout the world. However, they do concede ethnicity is very valuable indeed. Ethnicity includes languages, belief systems, clothing, food and the ways of a people that distinguishes them from other groups.

The Legacy continues on the subject of the re-introduction of Africans to America; in the form of slavery: Africans had a form of slavery and so did most of the ancient world—it was a way of life. However, the few African Chiefs had no idea what the Europeans had in mind for their fellow Africans that were being sold for a payment. This was not the usual method that the Europeans pursued. Most Africans were caught in traps, and kidnapped when walking alone in the jungle. Traps were set and Africans were caught in them like you would capture an animal from the jungle. The majority of Africans were stolen and very few were bought from tribal leaders. Slavery in Africa was very different from the slavery that was to come in America. When a tribe in Africa won a battle with an enemy tribe, the losers belonged to the winning tribe. The losing tribe could live and marry into the winning tribe, and become a Leader. There was nothing to stop the progress one could make within the winning tribal group. And of course, there was no problem with color as they were all the same or similar pigmentation. Slaves had to be very strong and determined to survive although slavery was made into a lifetime of bondage. God arranged in His time to free them. After all the Israelites were enslaved to the Egyptians for over 400 hundred years. From when Portugal and Spain began to steal Africans from Africa; slavery for the African Americans was also over 400 years. God in His own justification system saw to it that Israel was avenged, and thereby, it was necessary for Africans to suffer as they had turned away from God as the Israelites had done.

The Legacy continues: African Americans/Blacks after slavery to the present. Involves the lives of many people of color and their plight in life. Blacks were homeless and displaced and being told to live differently. Now they had to find a house, work and make money. This was new as the masters always provided a place to live and the work was automatic, without any pay! They had to struggle to get some form of education and to find employment.

The Legacy continues: African Americans had their faith in God and the Black church. The church has been an ever-present mainstay in the lives African Americans during and after bondage. The people believed that God would make a way for them one day. And He did. God made it possible for President Abraham Lincoln to write the Emancipation Proclamation in 1862. The Congress and Senate passed this legal document that re-united the union, the fact that the slaves were freed was a side issue. Thank you Lord Jesus for the blessings and the privilege of being free. Author's Note: When I was a child my parents use to tell me that I had to be better than any student in my classes. I never understood the reason for this, but today I do understand. It should never have been this way but it was and still is in many instances even today. In order to get promotions an African American has to be better by far.

Remember the committee meeting of Texaco leaders, and the laughing joke about "the black jelly beans always being stuck at the bottom." That was not funny and I am glad they had to pay a large fine and promote the worthy candidates. That is only one small example of inadequate treatment that remains in many areas of America to this day. The Texaco company paid out millions of dollars to these Black employees for a settlement! Some of the obstacles and hurdles placed in the way of Blacks have been overcome, conquered and "jumped over" one way or another. It is very difficult to keep good people down, and for the most part, Blacks, African Americans are hard working, good parents and dedicated. However, many Blacks or African Americans do not know their own history. Therefore, whatever is said about the group is sometimes readily accepted. Many educational institutions have removed Black History from their curriculums. This author will give an example of a few of the inventors and their inventions. Listed are just a few of the African American inventors and their contributions and/or discoveries that were made in America.

Prominent Figures From Historical Times

George Washington Carver
Produced over 300 products from the peanut. For example peanut butter and peanut products, which include stains and paints, printers, ink, axle grease and cooking oil. He also discovered over 118 products from the sweet potatoes. Dr. Carver further discovered 75 products from the pecan that we are still using in America today. He also taught the planters about crop rotation.

124

Dr. Benjamin Banneker
Inventor of the almanac and the clock. He was a scientist and an inventor. Washington, D.C. owes a great debt to the wonderful talents of Dr. Benjamin Banneker. When the architect L'enfant was disgruntled with the procedures and progress of the plaza that was being built he packed his blueprints and left. However, Banneker memorized the exact layout of the plaza and finished the work that L'enfant began. For all of Banneker's diligence and perseverance there is a very short street with his name on it, but L'enfant's name is all over D.C. and the D.C. plaza is named for him. Somehow it seems that no matter how much an African American does it is not "good enough."

Carter G. Woodson
Organized the first Negro history Week Celebration on the second week of February in 1926. The week long celebration eventually became a month long celebration, which is now known as Black History Month.

Buffalo Soldiers
This was a nickname given to African Americans soldiers of the 10th regiment. There were several African American regiments created during the Civil War to fight alongside the Union Army. After the war congress established the first peacetime all-Black regiment within the regular U.S. army called the "Buffalo Soliders".

Jesse Owens
Broke four world records in one afternoon at the Big Ten Championships on May 25, 1935. A year later, he upstaged Adolf Hitler by winning four gold medals (100m, 200m, 4x100m relay and long jump) at the 1936 Olympics in Berlin.

James Weldon Johnson
In 1900 he wrote with his brother the song "Lift Ev'ry Voice and Sing" on the occasion of Lincoln's birthday. The song became immensely popular in the Black community and became known as the "Negro National Anthem."

The African American Advisors to President Franklin D. Roosevelt
They were called the Black Brain Trust.

Frederick Eversley
African American sculptor. Created a stainless steel sculpture of two wings—like shapes framed by neon lights at the entrance to the Miami International Airport.

Crispus Attucks
His father was African and his mother was a Nantucket Indian. In 1770 he became the first casualty of the American Revolution when he was shot and killed in what became known as the Boston Massacre.

W.E.B. DuBois
Became the first African American to earn a PhD. from Harvard. He is perhaps best known for his work in founding the National Association for the Advancement of Colored people in 1909 and helping it to become the country's single most influential organization for African Americans.

Louis Latimer
The only African American engineer/scientist member of the elite Edison Pioneers research and development organization. Until Latimer's process for making carbon filaments, Edison's light bulbs would burn only a few minutes. Latimer's filament burned for hours.

Dr. Charles Drew
Was the first Black awarded a PhD. from Columbia University. He invented blood storage and created the first blood bank. He invented plasma—a method of separating and storing blood plasma allowing it to be dehydrated for later use.

Garrett Augustus Morgan
Invented a smoke hood in 1916 that he used to rescue several men trapped by an explosion in tunnels under Lake Erie. The U.S. Army

incorporated it into the gas mask, which was used to protect soldiers from chlorine fumes during W.W.I. He later refined this invention. He also invented an early version of a 3-way traffic signal that featured automated STOP and GO signs.

Matthew Henson
A Black explorer, accompanied Admiral Robert E. Peary on the first successful expedition to the North Pole in 1909. It has been stated that it was he and not Peary that placed the U.S. flag at the North Pole. However, because he was second in line to Peary, he was not given the recognition that he deserved.

Elijah McCoy
The son of escaped slaves from Kentucky; he was born in Canada and educated in Scotland. Settling in Detroit, Michigan, he invented a type of lubricator for steam engines (patented 1872) and established his own manufacturing company. During his lifetime he acquired 57 patents.

Norbert Rillieux
Born the son of a French planter and a slave woman in New Orleans, he was educated in France. Returning to the US he developed an evaporator for refining sugar, which he patented in 1846. Rillieux's evaporation technique is still used in the sugar industry and in the manufacture of soap and other products.

Benjamin O. Davis, Jr.
Became the first African American general in the U.S. Air Force in 1954.

Mr. George Crum
Inventor of the potato chip in 1853. While working as a Chef at a restaurant a customer requested French fries. When they were served he sent them back they were too thick, and too soft. Mr. Crum sliced the potatoes very thinly, fried them extra hard and added a small amount of salt. The American potato chip was born.

Bessie Coleman
A civil aviator, she was the first female pilot of African American descent to hold an international pilot's license. She became a media sensation when she launched herself as a stunt flyer under the moniker of "Queen Bess".

Jan Matzeliger
Invented the shoe lasting machine that connected the sole of the shoes to the upper portion. This process was usually done by hand, which was a slow and tedious process. The machine revolutionized the shoe making industry.

Paul Cuffee
Philanthropist, ship captain and devout Quaker. He transported 38 Free Blacks to Sierra Leone, Africa in 1815 in hopes of establishing Western Africa. He founded the first integrated school in Westport, Massachusetts in 1797.

George Ruffin & Richard Greener
In 1869, George Ruffin was the first Black person to graduate from the Harvard Law School (this was only a few years after the Civil War). Richard Greener also graduated from Harvard and in 1870 he became a lawyer, educator, and distinguished U.S. Consul and Diplomat.

These Blacks were able to be successful at a time when Blacks were denied any rights as American citizens. Think of what Blacks could do today if they were to become interested in education and dedicated to modeling themselves after these fine heroes from the past. African Americans have made major contributions to America and to the world. Past and present inventors are still inventing and America is still the recipient. One would have to look far and wide (most of the time) to see that the proper recognition has been forthcoming as it relates to Blacks' or African Americans' inventions or discoveries.

Modern Black Inventors and Contributors

Dr. Patricia Bath
The right to sight program: Dr. Bath is a noted Ophthalmologist. She also invented a laser phaco probe that was more comfortable and allowed for a more accurate procedure than previous methods for removing cataracts.

Dr. Mark Dean
Worked at IBM—he holds 9 P.C. patents, and holds a total of 20 patents. He led the team that developed the one-Gigahertz chip which contains one million transistors and has limitless potential.

Dr. Phillip Emeagwali
Known as the "Bill Gates of Africa!" He invented the world's fastest computers. He is also called 'the father of the Internet'. He has a Bell Laboratories Prize and the Nobel Prize for his work with computers. His inventions include predicting the likelihood and effects of global warming. The fastest computers perform at 3.1 billion calculations per second.

Ms. Valerie Thomas
Invented the "landsat" Satellite which shows illusions. It is able to send images into space. Invented 3-Dimensional images and worked for NASA. She also developed real-time computer data systems.

Dr. James West
90% of microphones in use today came from Dr. West's invention. He invented the electrets microphone transistors and the micro-electro acoustic transducer electrets microphones while working at Bell Labs. They are small, lightweight, accurate and reliable.

Frederick McKinley Jones
Invented the refrigeration machines used on long truck hauling machines. He developed a roof-mounted refrigeration unit. Mr. Jones made over 60 inventions, 40 of which were in the refrigeration

area. These cooling systems allow trucks to deliver frozen foods to the stores and the food stays fresh.

Mr. John Henry Thompson
He was a computer programmer and invented many software products. He invented the lingo programmer, a scripting language that renders visuals in computer programs. He also invented Macromedia to create multi-media content and applications combining computer programming language with visual arts.

Dr. Shirley Jackson
Modern day researcher, invented the portable fax, touchtone phones, solar cell phones, fiber optic cables to run cables underwater and around the world, the caller I.D. and call waiting, while heading Bell Laboratories (hopefully Dr. Jackson is related to the Jackson's from Florida).

Dr. Ben Carson
The head of Neurosurgery at Johns Hopkins Hospital in Baltimore, Maryland. He made medical history in 1987 when he was flown to Ulm, Germany to separate Siamese twins joined at the head. Carson is a Christian and was reared by a God-fearing mother. Her words of encouragement for her two boys were, "to be as good as everyone else and be better." Dr. Carson excelled in his field, and most importantly he prays prior to performing his surgeries.

Dr. Ralph J. Bunche
In 1950 he became the first African American to win the Nobel Peace Prize. While Under Secretary of the United Nations he negotiated the four armistice agreements that halted the Arab-Israeli War in 1948.

Mae C. Jemison
A physicist and NASA astronaut, she became the first African American woman to travel in space when she went into orbit aboard the Space Shuttle Endeavour on September 12, 1992. Jemison says she

was inspired by M. L. King Jr., "King's dream wasn't an elusive fantasy but a call to action."

These are examples of present day contributions made by African Americans. It is evident that there are many brilliant geniuses in the African American ethnic group. It makes one wonder if many young Blacks who have lost their lives could have invented the cure for cancer or some other serious disease. It has been proven that when given an opportunity for a good education, African Americans tend to flourish and excel. Having Christian, loving parents, many Blacks gained economic success, often with help from the church.

The Black church and faith has brought this group thus far, and with God's grace and guidance we will continue to be progressive and entrepreneurs into this new century. The church has been the stalwart for the black family. A refuge during slavery, it was a haven after slavery, and is a beacon for modern day families. This has been the main source from which African Americans or Blacks were able to gain spiritual power, and strength to continue to strive.

The modern Black church (in this author's opinion) has lost some of what it used to have in years past. Meaning that not all Black churches have retained the traditions they were once known for. There needs to be a renewing of commitment to reach out into the community to be of service to church members whenever the need arises. The Black church has always been a safe harbor for the community to find peace and comfort from the 'storms of life,' but some Black churches seem to have isolated themselves from the local community. The Black churches of the past were the traditional meeting places and often times the place for community voting—in other words, they were an integral part of the Black community. But despite this trend, there are some churches that do adhere to the traditions that the Black church has been noted for in the past; which includes community involvement and being there for the people. There is one thing that I do know for sure and that is no matter what man does, God is still in control!

Some of the many atrocities that African Americans have endured and in some cases overcome:

The Little Rock Nine
A group of African American students who were enrolled in Little Rock Central High School in 1957. In the ensuing Little Rock Crisis, the students were initially prevented from entering the racially segregated school by Arkansas Governor Orval Faubus. President Eisenhower called out the Arkansas N.G. but they refused to allow the Black students to enter the school. Next, the President called out the Federal N.G. and they permitted the students to enter the school. This scene made history.

Loving vs. Virginia (1967)
A landmark civil rights case in which the United States Supreme Court, by a 9-0 vote, declared Virginia's anti-miscegenation statute, the "Racial Integrity Act of 1924", unconstitutional, thereby overturning Pace vs. Alabama (1883) and ending all race-based legal restrictions on marriage in the United States.

The Tuskegee Syphilis Experiment
Was a clinical study conducted between 1932 and 1972 in Tuskegee, Alabama, by the U.S. Public Health Service, to study the natural progression of untreated syphilis. Investigators enrolled in the study impoverished African American sharecroppers from Macon County, Ala. infected them with syphilis. They were never told they had syphilis, nor were they ever treated for it. According to the Centers for Disease Control, the men were told they were being treated for "bad blood," a local term used to describe several illnesses.

The Tuskegee Airmen
A group of African American pilots who fought in World War II, the Tuskegee Airmen were the first African American military aviators in the United States armed forces. During World War II, African Americans in many U.S. states still were subject to racist, so-called Jim Crow laws. The American military was racially segregated, as was much

of the federal government. The Tuskegee Airmen were subject to racial discrimination, both within and outside the army. Despite these adversities, they trained and flew with distinction.

Emmett Till
An African American boy who at 14 years old was murdered in Mississippi after reportedly flirting with a white woman. Till was from Chicago, Illinois visiting his relatives in the Mississippi Delta region when he spoke to 21-year-old Carolyn Bryant, the married proprietor of a small grocery store. Several nights later, Bryant's husband Roy and his half-brother J. W. Milam, arrived at Till's great-uncle's house where they took Till, transported him to a barn, beat him and gouged out one of his eyes, before shooting him through the head and disposing of his body in the Tallahatchie River, weighting it with a 70-pound cotton gin fan tied around his neck with barbed wire. His body was discovered and retrieved from the river three days later. The White men involved were found innocent of Till's murder by an all-White jury!

Shirley Sherrod
Because of remarks she made that were taken out of context by Andrew Breithart, Ms. Sherrod was asked to resign her position with the U.S.D.A. Comments were made about her without anyone knowing the full content of her video presentation. When the full presentation was viewed everyone was apologetic. She was offered her job back.

There is a great (so-called) racial divide still in America, with the vestiges of slavery and "Jim Crow" racism continuing in one form or another. It would seem obvious that African Americans are citizens and cannot be controlled by hatred when there is so much love to be shared. Why would a strong, independent nation like ours become subject to old patterns of division and hatred? This does not make any sense at all to a thinking, logical, and rational American. However, the racists, the bigots (like the KKK), and some skin-heads that hate are still doing damage to people of color in America. There should be none of this going on but it is. These type haters hide and wait for darkness to do their evil deeds. Bigotry is not limited to the south anymore, now it is all across the nation. Cross burnings, racist graffiti, threats and intimidations are going on nationwide. These tactics did not work in past years and with Gods' help they will not succeed in this modern generation.

The Legacy continues: For some Blacks, the "chains on the mind" syndrome is as real as the chains that were on the body during slavery. This means that there has to be a re-indoctrination concerning the wondrous historical contributions supplied by people from Africa. Perhaps the "playing field is not quite level" but it is not as far out of kilter as it was years ago. There is still hope and we all must pray and hope for a just and equal nation, which can only come about with love for the Lord Jesus Christ and putting Him first in our lives, from the President to the lowly street cleaner. America, we can do this, yes we can!

Americans living in this land of the free and home of the brave, all have much to be grateful for. There has been much progress toward "racial peace," but there is still lots left to do. Especially, there is a need for solidarity in African American communities. Blacks need to get back to a sense of community. It is not that integration is a "bad" thing; however, the sense of peoplehood/community no longer seems to exist. This book is dedicated to all of my Black and White brothers and sisters in the name of the Lord Jesus Christ. There should be a sense of added pride and a sense of thankfulness for the many contributions made by "our" forefathers from Africa to the world and to America. Blacks through the years have made tremendous journeys that have impacted the world. "Looking back 'into history', While Moving Forward" into the Twenty First Century! May God richly bless each one of you that reads my book—Thank You!

Acknowledgments

First and foremost I want to honor my Lord and Savior Jesus Christ for all of His blessings, mercy and love in my life. Thanks, Lord Jesus, for helping me to complete this book, finally.

To Mr. Homer Lee Jackson, Sr., my beloved father, my heartfelt thanks for all his prayers and confidence in me no matter what my endeavors in life. My father is now with the Lord, but his loving memory will be forever in my heart.

Thanks to my mother, Ella Lee Jackson, for her support and love.

To my brother Bishop Robert Lee Jackson the pastor of Acts Full Gospel Church in Oakland, California, a special thanks for all of your prayers.

Thanks to my beautiful daughter Michelle Yuvienco, for your gracious support and gentle encouragement: "Finish the book Mom! How much did you do today? Complete the book, Mom. Hurry up!"

I am grateful to my god-sister, Jeanette Stoneham, for helping to organize this book. My gratitude also goes to my brothers in Christ, Gary Benefiel and Al Diaz at the Christ Community Fellowship Church in Walla Walla, Washington, for your proofreading.

Stephen Docherty is my publisher on this edition of *The Legacy*. He has helped to change the format of the book made it an easier read. He has done a superb job, I am eternally grateful to him for his wonderful expertise. Stephen loves the Lord Jesus and is a wonderful human. I hope to visit the United Kingdom to meet him in person, and see my friend Mr. William (Bill) Grimke-Drayton.

To my granddaughter, Claudia Vargas, thanks for helping with the sizing of the front cover, and thanks to her sister Jocelyn and my god daughter their mom, Ines Arenas, for helping with the book.

To my oldest daughter Yolanda Yuvienco, she did an excellent job of editing this edition, for which I am eternally grateful.

Thanks to my wonderful Black History students from the University of Alaska, in 1994, who encouraged me early on in the writing of this book.

To my present Pastor Rev/Dr W.G.Hardy, Jr., Highland Christian Center. Pastor is a Godly man and he preaches from the Bible. I am very happy to be a member. I know that I am "in the right place."

To my past Pastors Eddie Jordan and the late Dr. Leo Scott from Abilene, Texas, for their words of encouragement and prayers during the writing process.

To my past late Pastor Willie B. Smith, Associate Minister Dapo Sobomehin, and new Associate Minister Benny Carson Sr. at, The Church of The Good Shepherd in Portland, Oregon. Thanks to all of you for your kindness and prayers for my success.

To my past Anchorage, Alaska pastor Wilbert Mickens, Jr. Thanks for your prayers and support. I am praying that one day soon the Educational Foundation will finally be completed to help deserving college students (please remember the Foundation is to be named in my honor!) I appreciate my church members for being so supportive and loving. I am grateful to God that I have such a wonderful church family!

References

Forward: The Legacy

Moore, Richard B., The Name "Negro its Origin and Evil Uses p. 13

Chapter 1

The Origin of Humankind

[1] Genesis 1:26-27
[2] Ibid 2:7
[3] Ibid 2:11-14
[4] Ibid 11:6-9

Chapter 2

The Birth and Genealogy of Jesus

Dr James Peebles (Publisher) Felder, Cain Hope (Editor) The Original African Heritage Study Bible

[1] Matthew 1:1-16
[2] Isaiah 53:1-12
[3] Matthew 1:18
[4] Ibid 2:1-3
[5] p. 1377 (OAHSB)
[6] Daniel 7:9
[7] p. 4 (OAHSB)
[8] Revelation 1:14-15
[9] p. vii (OAHSB)
[10] p. xv (OAHSB)
[11] p. xii (OAHSB)
[12] p. 3 (OAHSB)
[13] p.3 (OAHSB)
[14a] p. 1814 (a) (OAHSB)
[14b] p. 1814 (b) (OAHSB)
[15] Peebles, James W. Preface p. 1 (OAHSB)
[16] p. 4 (OAHSB)
[17] p. 334 (OAHSB)
[18] Galatians 3:28
[19] Genesis 16:11-17
[20] p.1-8 (OAHSB)

Chapter 3

Civilization in Africa

[1] Lerone Bennett Jr., Before the Mayflower p. 5 (a)
[2] Ibid. p. 5 (b)
[3] Ibid. p. 32
[4] Ibid. p. 5-6
[5] Bennett, Lerone Jr. p. 24
[6] James, George G.M, Stolen Legacy p. 7
[7] Rogers p. 17 Africa's Gift to America
[8] Ibid. p. 17-18
[9] Gerald Horne, Thinking and Rethinking U.S. History p. 19
[10] Carol Berkin et al, American Voices p. 19
[11] Bennett p. 5-6
[12] Ibid p. 6
[13] Rogers p. 14
[14] Jackson, Man, God, and Civilization p. 284
[15] Van Sertima p. 17 They came before Columbus
[16] Rogers p. 16
[17] Rogers on Dr. Wiener p. 16
[18] Rogers p. 18
[19] Bennett chapters 16 & 17
[20] Rogers p. 7-8
[21] Ibid p. 11
[22] Ibid p. 46-47 Rogers on Jackson
[23] Rogers on Dr. Wiener p. 78
[24] Ibid p. 59 (a)
[25] Ibid p. 59 (b)
[26] Van Sertima p. 78
[27] Ibid p. 17
[28] Ibid p. 15-17
[29] Van Sertima p. 256

Chapter 4

The Sociology of Race and Ethnicity

[1] Macionis, John J. p. 348
[2] Ibid p. 448
[3] Ibid p. 348
[4] Ibid p. 347
[5] Ibid p. 447

Chapter 5

The Re-introduction of Blacks to Americas

[1] John Hope Franklin and Alfred A. Moss Junior., From Slavery to Freedom. p. 32-33

[2] Horne, Gerald p. 55

[3] Ibid p. 61

[4] Rogers p. 31 From Superman to Man

[5] Bennett, Lerone Jr. p. 136

[6] Horne, Gerald p. 59

[7] Jackson, John G. p. 306

[8] Franklin & Moss p. 106

[9] Bernard, Jesse Marriage and Family Among Negroes, p. 103-104

[10] Lynch, Willie, The Willie Lynch Law

[11] Van Sertima p. 75

[12] Grimke-Drayton, William (reprint)w/permission 2007

[13] Rogers p. 74 From Superman to Man

[14] Billingsley, Andrew, Dr. p. 61 Black Families in White America

[15] Franklin & Moss p. 103-104

Chapter 6

The Black Family from 1865-Present

[1] Andrew Billingsley, Black Families in White America p. 71
[2] John Hope Franklin and Alfred A. Moss Junior, From Slavery to Freedom p. 208
[3] Ibid p. 208
[4] Ibid p. 209
[5] Ibid p. 215
[6] Ollin P. Moyd, Redemption in Black Theology p. 201
[7] Macionis, John J. Sociology p. 467

Chapter 7

The Black Church—The Black Religion

The Original African Heritage Study Bible

[1] Psalm 68:21
[2] P. 1816
[3] Ibid 1816
[4] Ibid 1816
[5] Jackson, John G. p. 261
[6] Preface p. 1
[7] Rogers p. 36
[8] Ibid p. 37
[9] Ibid p. 41
[10] Seaton #14 Ibid p. 125
[11] Franklin & Moss p. 124-125
[12] Ibid p. 94
[13] Franklin & Moss p. 125
[14] Cleage, Albert B. p. 5 Black Christian Nationalism New Direction for the Black Church
[15] Cone, James p. 79 Black Theology and Black Power
[16] Cleage, Albert B. p. 132
[17] Ibid p. 135-136
[18] Cone, James p. 159
[19] Ibid p. 159
[20] Paris, Peter J. p. 99 The Social Teaching of the Black Churches
[21] Paris p. 100
[22] Browder, Anthony p. 3 From the Browder Files
[23] Ibid p. 3
[24] Ibid p. 3-4
[25] Welsing. Cress, Frances p. 170 The Isis Papers
[26] Ibid p. 170
[27] Ibid p. 170
[28] Ibid p. 171

Bibliography

Akbar, Na'im. Chains and Images of Psychological Slavery. Jersey City, NJ: New Mind Productions, 1991

Bennett, Lerone, Jr., Before the Mayflower: A History of the Negro in America (1619-1962) Johnson Publishing Co., Inc., Chicago, Ill Baltimore, MD.,1962.

Berkin, Carol, et. al. American Voices. Glenville, IL: Scott Foresman, 1992.

Bernard, Jessie. Marriage and Family Among Negroes. Englewood Cliffs, NJ: Prentice-Hall, Inc., 1966.

Billingsley, Andrew. Black Families in White America. Englewood Cliffs, NJ: Prentice-Hall, Inc., 1968.

Birnbaum, Norman, and Gertrude Lenzer. Sociology and Religion, A Book of Reading. Englewood Cliffs, NJ: Prentice-Hall, Inc., 1969.

"Black Church Celebrates Bicentennial." Anchorage Daily News, 7 Anchorage, Alaska, November 1992, 8(F).

Botkins, B.A. Lay My Burdens Down. Chicago, IL: University of Chicago Press, 1945.

Browder, Anthony T. From the Browder File. Washington, D.C.: The Institute of Karmic Guidance, 1989.

Brown, Richard D., and Stephen G. Rabe. Slavery in American Society. Lexington, MA: D.C. Heath and Co., 1976.

Carmichael, Stokely, and Charles V. Hamilton. Black Power, The Politics of Liberation in America. New York, NY: New York Vintage Books, 1967.

Cary, Lorene. Black Ice. New York, NY: Alfred A. Knopf, 1991.

Chapman, Abraham. Black Voices, An Anthology of Afro-American Literature. New York, NY: Times Mirror (Mentor Books from New American Library), 1968.

"Chromosome trail leads to African Adam." Anchorage Daily News, 26 May, 1995, 1(A). Anchorage, Alaska

Clark, Kenneth B. Dark Ghetto. New York, NY: Harper and Row, 1965.

Cleage, Albert B. Black Christian Nationalism New Directions for the Black Church. Detroit, MI: Luxor Publisher of the Pan-African Orthodox Christian Church, 1972.

Cone, James H. Black Theology and Black Power. New York, NY: Seabury Press, 1969.

Liberation: A Black Theology of Liberation. New York, NY: J.B. Lippincott Co., 1970.

For My People, Black Theology and the Black Church. Maryknoll, NY: Orbis Books, 1991.

God of the Oppressed. New York, NY: Seabury Press, 1975.

Cress-Welsing, Frances. The Isis Papers. Chicago, IL: Third World Press, 1991.

Davidson, Basil. The African Past. New York, NY: Grosset and Dunlap, 1964.

Drake, St Clair, and Horace Cayton. Black Metropolis, A Study of Negro Life in a Northern City. New York, NY: Harper and Row, 1945.

DuBois, W.E.B. The Negro American Family. Cambridge, MA: M.I.T. Press, 1909.

Elkins, Stanley M. Slavery, A Problem in American Institutional and Intellectual Life. New York, NY: Grosset and Dunlap, Inc., 1963.

Felder, Cain, editor. The Original African Heritage Study Bible (King James Version). Nashville, TN: James C. Winston Co., 1993.

Felder, Cain Hope. Stony the Road We Trod. Minneapolis, MN: Fortress Press, 1991.

Troubling Biblical Waters. Race, Class and Family. Maryknoll, NY: Orbis Books, 1992.

Franklin, John Hope and Alfred A. Moss, Jr. From Slavery to Freedom. 6th ed. New York, NY: McGraw Hill, Inc., 1988.

Frazier, E. Franklin. The Black Bourgeoisie. Glencoe, IL: The Free Press, 1957. Black Bourgeoisie, The Rise of a New Middle Class in the United States. New York, NY: Collier Books (The Free Press), 1962.

The Free Negro Family. Nashville, TN: Fisk University Press, 1932.

The Negro Church in America. New York, NY: Schocken Books, 1974.

The Negro Family in the United States. Chicago, IL: University of Chicago Press, 1948.

Freund, Julien. The Sociology of Max Weber. New York, NY: Vintage Books Random House, 1969.

Grimke-Drayton, William (permission given to print December, 2007) Harrison, Bob. When God Was Black. Concord, CA: Bob Harrison Ministries International, 1978.

Herskovits, Melville. The Myth of the Negro Past. Boston, MA: Beacon press, 1958.

Holly, Alonzo Potter. God and the Negro, Synopsis of God and the Negro of the Biblical Record of the Race of Ham. Nashville, TN: National Baptist Board, 1937.

Horne, Gerald. Thinking and Rethinking US History. New York, NY: The Council of Interracial Books for Children, Inc., 1988.

Hough, Joseph C., Jr. Black Power and White Protestants, A Christian Response to the New Negro Pluralism. New York, NY: Oxford University Press, 1968.

Jackson, John G. Introduction to African Civilization Citadel Press, Carol Publishing group, New York, New York, 1970

Man, God and Civilization. Secaucus, NJ: Citadel Press, 1972.

Jackson, Robert L. Church Building Through Evangelism. Columbus, GA: Brentwood Christian Press, 1989.

James, G.M George, Stolen Legacy, African World Press, Trenton N.J. 1992

Johnson, James Weldon. God's Trombones, Seven Negro Sermons in Verse. New York, New York: Penguin Books, 1990.

Kardiner, Abram, and Lionel Ovesey. The Mark of Oppression. New York, NY: W.W. Norton Co., 1951.

Lincoln, C. Eric. The Black Church Since Frazier. New York, NY: Schocken Books, 1974.

The Negro Pilgrimage in America. New York, NY: Bantam Books, Pathfinder Editors, 1967.

Lynch, William, The Willie Lynch Letter: "The Making of a Slave," FCN Publishing Co., Reprinted, 2005

Macionis, John J. Sociology. 7th ed. Prentice Hall, Englewood Cliffs, NJ: 1999.

Marx, Gary T. Protest and Prejudice, A Study of Belief in the Black Community.

New York, NY: Harper Torch books (Harper and Row), 1969.

Moore, Richard B. The Name "Negro" and its Evil Uses, Black Classic Press, Baltimore, MD:1960

Moyd, Olin P. Redemption In Black Theology. Valley Forge, PA: 1979.

Paris, Peter J. The Social Teaching of the Black Church. Philadelphia, PA: Fortress Press, 1985.

Parsons, Talcott, and Kenneth B. Clark. The Negro American. Boston, MA: Beacon Press, 1966.

Pettigrew, Thomas F. A Profile of the Negro American. Princeton, NJ: D. Van Norstrand Co., 1964.

Pinkney, Alphonso. Black Americans. Englewood Cliffs, NJ: Prentice-Hall, 1969.

Quarles, Benjamin. The Negro in the Making of America. London: Collier Books (Division of Macmillan Publishing Co., Inc.), 1969.

Roberts, J. Deotis. Liberation and Reconciliation, A Black Theology. Philadelphia, PA: Westminster Press, 1971.

Rogers, J.A. Africa's Gift to America, The Afro-American in the Making and Saving of the United States. New York, NY: Helga M. Rogers, 1961.

Sex and Race, Volumes I through III. New York, NY: Helga M. Rogers, 1944.

World's Greatest Men of Color, Volumes I and II. New York, NY: Collier Books, 1964.

"Pope Begs Forgiveness for Slave Trade." Oakland Tribune, 7 March, 1992. Smith, Wallace Charles. The Church in the Life of the Black Family. Valley Forge, PA: Judson Press, 1985.

Stallings, James O. Telling the Story, Evangelism in Black Churches. Valley Forge, PA: Judson Press, 1988.

Stampp, Kenneth M. The Peculiar Institution, Slavery in the Ante-Bellum South. New York, NY: Vintage Books (Division of Random House), 1956.

Staples, Robert. The Black Family, Essays and Studies. Belmont, CA: Wadsworth Publishing Co., 1991.

Stewart, Warren H., Sr. Interpreting God's Word in Black Preaching. Valley Forge, PA: Judson Press, 1984.

The Holy Bible (King James Version). Camden, NJ: Thomas Nelson, Inc., 1970.

Van Sertima, Ivan. They Came Before Columbus. New York, NY: Random House, 1976.

Washington, Booker T. Up From Slavery. New York, NY: Doubleday and Company (Bantam Books), 1959.

Washington, Joseph J. Black Religion, The Negro and Christianity in the United States. Boston, MA: Beacon press, 1964.

Washington, Preston Robert. God's Transforming Spirit, Black Church Renewal. Valley Forge, PA: Jedson Press, 1988.

Weber, Max. The Sociology of Religion. Boston, MA: Beacon Press, 1956.

Webster's Collegiate Dictionary, Tenth Edition, Springfield, MA: Merriam-Webster, Inc., 1988.

Wegener, Alfred. The Origin of Continents and Oceans. New York: Dover Press. 1966

Wiener, Leo. Africa and The Discovery of America. Brooklyn, NY: A&B Book Company, 1992, reprinted.

Williams, Chancellor. The Destruction of Black Civilization. Chicago, IL: Third World Press, 1974.

About the Author

Fredi Jackson attended U.C. Berkeley in the 1960s and is a graduate of the International Seminary with a PhD. She is now retired and works for herself, providing services for others. An ordained minister, Fredi is dedicated to working for God. Her faith is very deep and she knows that she can do nothing without the Lord Jesus in her life. Fredi is a mother, grandmother and great-grandmother. As well as writing academic books she also writes children's stories.

41232017R00102

Made in the USA
Charleston, SC
25 April 2015